To Mary Ann Keeler
with warm personal regards
Louis Redstone
March '76

ART IN ARCHITECTURE

FRONTISPIECE

THE CHICAGO CIVIC CENTER, CHICAGO, ILLINOIS. ***Architects:*** **C. F. Murphy Associates; Skidmore, Owings & Merrill; and Loebl Schlossman Bennett & Dart.** ***Artist:*** **Pablo Picasso, steel sculpture, 50′ high; 1967.** ***Photographer:*** **Ezra Stoller Associates.**

ART IN ARCHITECTURE

 Library of Congress Catalog Card Number: 68-13098

4567890 HDBP 765

Photographic layout and design by William A. Bostick

Design consultant: Susan Keig

To
my sons Daniel and Eliel
and to other future architects
to encourage art as a part
of living environment.

INTRODUCTION BY JACQUES LIPCHITZ

Dear Louis,

As you know, my father was a building contractor; in reality, a very able architect without a diploma. When I was around fourteen years old I was completely involved in sculpture. Probably trying to keep me away from it my father started to tell me that *architecture* is the queen of the plastic arts and not sculpture. Of course I was not listening to his sayings, being so involved in my desire to be a sculptor. Later on in Paris, having difficulties with my art, I started to think about my father's sermons and began to study architecture in order to understand what my father meant.

As a result of my studies I came to the conclusion that my father was right. But why? Only because architecture is a summary of all the plastic arts. However, if we take away some parts of this complex, would architecture still be the queen of the plastic arts? My answer is no, because if we would take that for granted, we could come to an absurdum, for example: that some nicely built shack is of greater plastic significance than a sculpture by Michelangelo! For me a building without sculpture and painting is simply housing, it could be a very ingenious harmonious housing but it is not more than housing and cannot pretend to be the queen of the plastic arts.

I vividly remember my arguments with Corbusier. He built a house and studio for me in Paris, long before he was known as a great architect. My house was ready in 1924. I think if I am not mistaken, it was the third he ever built. It was around this time or maybe in 1925 or 1926 that we were at Place St. Augustin in Paris discussing, as always, architecture. At that time the "Cercle Militaire," which was in front of us, was being finished. I remember I said to him "look at this building, that's architecture, very bad architecture, but nevertheless it is architecture. But what you are trying to do is only housing, very good housing, but only housing." Many years later he probably came to the conclusion that I was right because he started to introduce sculpture into his buildings, but his own sculpture. Being a poor sculptor and probably sensing it, his next step was to approach his architecture as a sculptor approaches his sculpture. Ronchamp is a result of this way of thinking. Even though it is a very interesting building, for me it is not a sculpture at all. It is wrong to think about sculpture in this way because it ignores the aims of sculpture and the nature of architecture.

This tendency of Corbusier's is reflected in some other buildings here and abroad. It is a kind of tendency which I find in contemporary architecture and for me it is a good sign because it shows an attraction toward sculpture in the mind of the architects, and in the long run the architects will become what they always were: "Maitres d'oeuvres." It is to say, like conductors of orchestras, letting every musician play his instrument to produce the symphony of our time.

It will require great humility on their part and I am convinced that it will come.

Yours as ever,

Jacques

FOREWORD BY ROBERT L. DURHAM, FAIA

The profession of architecture and the public it serves are indeed fortunate that one of its distinguished members has seen fit to produce a book on art and architecture.

This book is especially timely now when we are entering a creative period of rebuilding our cities and of planning new ones. Now is a time of great opportunity for architects and artists to collaborate and combine their talents and efforts to create a living environment where the arts will play a meaningful role in the life of the individual and the community.

This book is directed to the architectural profession as well as to the general public. The architects will find in this publication a wealth of material on the integration of the arts, showing a wide cross section of good examples in the United States and in many countries the world over.

For those architects who are interested in the arts, the book opens new vistas and an opportunity to get acquainted with the work of many young and talented artists, as well as with the recent commissions executed by internationally known artists. For the many architects who have been reluctant to use art in their buildings, the examples shown should encourage a reevaluation of their thinking on the integration of the arts in view of the growing interest on the part of the public and the individual client.

To laymen and the general public, this book will be a reassurance that art can enrich their lives when it is a part of their daily environment. The book will also help them understand contemporary developments here and abroad.

The importance that The American Institute of Architects attaches to this vital subject is indicated by the establishment in 1964 of the Committee on Collaborating Arts. This committee's primary objective is to encourage productive collaboration with artists and artisans, especially as related to the place of art in the urban environment.

Louis G. Redstone, author of this book, has made the integration of the arts a basic element in his philosophic approach to architecture. He practices what he preaches, and the majority of his buildings, private or public, reflect his successful collaboration with artists.

In its continuing effort to produce a climate conducive to fruitful collaboration between architect and artist, The American Institute of Architects takes pleasure in endorsing *Art in Architecture* to its membership and to the public it seeks to serve.

PREFACE BY LOUIS G. REDSTONE, FAIA

This book is written with a fervent hope that all the arts will take their rightful place again in the total environment of our reborn cities. The geometric patterns of our buildings, so characteristic of our machine-age period, more than ever before demand the human touch of the sculptor, the painter, and the craftsman.

The new techniques of construction available to most areas of the world and the closeness of the continents made possible by fast means of travel contribute greatly to the sameness of character of today's buildings. Any of the recent contemporary buildings could be placed in one country or another, without expressing any special regional character by itself.

A basic factor used by historians and archaeologists to interpret the life modes of past generations is man's creativeness as expressed in objects of both religious and utilitarian character. At the present time, there is much to indicate that the new art forms being evolved reflect the way of life of our generation. However, the tremendous impact and the rapidity of new and dramatic developments in science and technology influencing our way of life will force future historians to evaluate us not in terms of centuries but in terms of decades. The aim of this book is to stimulate and promote the integration of the arts in architecture by presenting the best current examples of architect-artist collaboration.

The examples chosen here will show that there is a beginning of an art renaissance in this country and in many parts of the world. A most hopeful sign is the lively interest that city, state, and Federal authorities are taking in allotting a percentage for art work in their building budgets.

Ironically enough, even in the depression days of the 1930s, the Federal government through the WPA inaugurated an extensive art program for government buildings. Presently New York, Philadelphia, and many other cities are following this policy. In private enterprise, large trust and insurance companies, banks, and various industrial concerns are assembling art collections and are commissioning meaningful art work for their buildings. Public interest is also growing steadily, as witnessed by the proliferation of art galleries.

The most significant phenomenon in developing public interest and appreciation of art related to architecture occurred at Expo 67 in Montreal, Canada. There, nearly every nation commissioned its best artists to create works of art to be integrated with the design of the pavilions. There can be no doubt that the impact on the millions of visitors from all parts of the globe will continue to generate further public interest. Because of its temporary and short-lived use, the representative examples of Expo 67 were not included in this book.

All these factors serve as a good beginning. However, greater efforts have to be made in other directions.

First, the architect must become the moving element in the promotion of art in his building. He must call on the artist or the craftsman at the very beginning of his preliminary conceptual sketches and design a space for murals, sculpture, or other art forms. Like any other element, these must become integral parts of the building without which something vital would be missing.

Second, the artists and craftsmen must familiarize themselves with technological advances and new materials. They also must consider the factors of scale and permanence in their work. They should be in closer contact with the architects and have some technical knowledge when designing such items as fountains which involve plumbing, electrical, and structural elements. Better communication between artists and architects would bring out available talented artists in our midst who are just waiting for a chance to work with architects.

Third, the groundwork has to be laid at the elementary educational level to prepare a young generation to become receptive to the benefits of art in everyday living. Thus, we shall raise a new generation which will demand and expect art forms as a matter of fact in their daily lives.

Most important of all, the architect has to be convinced himself before he can convince his clients that art is not a luxury.

In schools, historical murals and other art forms add to the background of students in the encouragement of art studies. In hospitals, art can have a therapeutic value for patients and their families. In public buildings, it reduces the pressures of the daily routine by focusing attention on provocative art forms. In shopping centers, it exposes great numbers of people to important works of art as well as to playful sculptures, which the children touch, climb, and enjoy. In city plazas and parks, works of art are a constant source of enjoyment for a multitude of people for whom this is often the only exposure to art, as well as a beginning for further interest and exploration.

Murals or sculptures are not the only elements representing the arts. Among other aspects of the arts are landscaping, fabrics, lighting, graphics, metal screens, furniture, and accessories.

I realize that it is not an easy task for an architect to specify art work as part of a building together with hardware and plumbing. There is constant pressure on the part of the client, whether he is an individual or a government agency, to omit anything from which he does not derive tangible physical comfort or profit.

Fundamentally, I think the additional cost is not the main deterring factor. It is the exaggerated emphasis that is put on physical values and the smaller emphasis on cultural values. People have accepted numerous additional costs of buildings, such as the costs for air conditioning, better and fancier plumbing, etc. We pay for all these items because we note tangible results. When cultural values are interpreted as essential to well-being, then the demand for art will become a "normal" requirement.

All this goes hand in hand with the war against "urban ugliness." The architect must become interested in the life of his community, take leadership, and work unselfishly for the betterment of his environment. Even though the profession of architecture is a full-time occupation, a certain part of the architect's time must be devoted to improving the living standards of his fellowmen. I repeat, there is a continuous "war" to be fought—the war against community ugliness. The architectural profession is heeding President Johnson's initial call to eradicate ugliness in all its aspects. Architects and city planners need to be in the forefront of this fight. Essential to this objective, I believe, is the integration of art in all of its forms in the daily life of the community.

The need to support all the arts was recognized by an act of Congress in September, 1965 when it established the National Foundation on the Arts and Humanities with its two branches, the National Endowment for the Arts and the National Endowment for the Humanities. Under the chairmanship of Roger L. Stevens, councils of experts to advise each endowment were set up by the Congress in 1964. The practical result was to give subsidies to sculptors, painters, poets, writers, and ballet companies to enable them to devote full time to creative works. Another hopeful sign in the support of creative artists is the projected planning of low-cost apartments and studios in New York City. This project is a joint venture of a private corporate fund and the National Council of the Arts. It should go a long way to provide many artists with good facilities in which to work and live.

A pilot project to provide studio space for local talented artists is being successfully carried out in Detroit, where it is known as The Common Ground of the Arts. A converted industrial loft in the inner city was divided into 20 studios for painters, sculptors, graphic artists, and photographers. Expanded facilities are provided when the need arises. A minimum rent is charged, the deficit being covered by private contributors. This group of artists could very well serve as a nucleus for developing similar centers in other parts of the city.

I am convinced that activities of this kind will strengthen the architect's role in the struggle to rejuvenate and revitalize our cities.

The purpose of this book is to acquaint the architects and the general public with most recent examples of the use of art in buildings. These examples represent a wide and varied cross section of types of buildings and of differing approaches to the use of art forms. These are the works of architects and artists, many of whom are young and known only in their own regions. The architect can readily see from the presented material that in many instances he may be able to find, if he seeks, able and competent artists in his own area.

There is no limit to the variety of possibilities in both art forms and materials which the architect can utilize. This book shows how brickwork, the age-old material, can be used as new sculptured forms by artists and architects alike.

The text is kept purposely to a minimum, with the major emphasis on visual illustrations. I have not attempted to delve into the complex philosophical aspects of the subject, as this has been covered in other publications.

It is my sincere hope that this book will, in some measure, encourage the architectural profession to advance the use of the arts in buildings and will stimulate the general public to become aware of the value of beauty in everyday life.

Acknowledgments

For preparing this material, I am indebted greatly to Wm. Dudley Hunt, Jr., publisher of the *AIA Journal*, whose encouragement and confidence in my project helped to bring it to fruition; to the many AIA chapters that spread the word about this project among their members and, in some instances, assembled and sent me the material; to the architectural offices throughout the country, which were very cooperative in forwarding the required information; to the national architectural societies of many countries around the world that printed my notice in their publications and helped with the assembling of the photographic materials from their members; and to the many artists here and abroad whose enthusiasm and cooperation made this work an event of joy and discovery. To Susanne Faulkner of the public relations department of Lincoln Center for the Performing Arts; to Robert Wells and Mrs. Maurice Rosenbaum, for the International Sculpture Symposium material; to Donald E. Wudtke, for the Golden Gateway Center material; to Bruce J. Reiss, deputy city manager, city of Fresno, for the Fresno data; to E. A. Van Name and Marvin Weill of the United Nations staff; to Mrs. Ilse Gerson of Marlborough-Gerson Gallery; to J. J. Beljon of Holland; to Mrs. Ruth Rivera Marin of Mexico for her assistance in assembling material on Mexican artists and architects; and to many companies and individuals too numerous to thank individually, my heartiest thanks and appreciation. I am especially indebted to my secretarial assistants and, above all, to my wife Ruth, whose endless hours and days spent as "right-hand secretary" made the effort an enjoyable experience.

TABLE OF CONTENTS

Part I:

United States and Canada

Part II:

Countries Around the World

Part I

United States and Canada

EDUCATIONAL BUILDINGS

It should be an exhilarating experience for the college student to walk through a well-planned campus plaza and be stimulated by works of art which reflect the searching efforts of our great and talented artists. The campus is an ideal place for the student to be exposed to art in all its forms, and an atmosphere of art thus becomes a necessary part of his life. There is a good possibility that many students, as future leaders, will have a strong influence in their communities in building a similar environment where art plays a significant role. The establishment of the artist-in-residence on many campuses should be a big factor in strengthening the continuity in art interest among students. This practice also gives the artist an opportunity to create large-scale work as part of the campus or school buildings.

The illustrations shown here give a great variety of approaches in the use of materials and in the relationship of the works of art to the buildings. In the dormitories at Yale University by Eero Saarinen, the concrete sculpture by Costantino Nivola becomes an integral part of the building. The same is true of the sculptured tower by Robert Engman in the Yale Art and Architecture Building designed by Paul Rudolph. In the case of UCLA the freestanding works of art such as the sculptures by Jacques Lipchitz and others become a part of the plaza development. Other examples illustrate the use of metal bas-reliefs on exterior surfaces, wood reliefs on interior walls, fountains, brick and mosaic murals both exterior and interior, concrete precast murals for exterior walls, and interior painted murals.

MORSE AND STILES DORMITORIES, YALE UNIVERSITY, NEW HAVEN, CONNECTICUT. *Architects*: Eero Saarinen & Associates. *Artist*: Costantino Nivola, concrete sculpture; 1962. *Photographer*: Balthazar Korab.

Reuben Nakian's conception of a university and the location of New York University itself were the inspiration for his design of the abstract sculpture. Nakian says, "I conceive the university as a nest. The students are fledglings, and once they are educated and civilized they fly away. Education is the freeing of the spirit. The setting through the trees of the park also made me think of wind-blown leaves."

The sculpture is designed to throw different patterns of shadows on the wall of the auditorium during different parts of the day and to create variations of the theme. The color, light and dark values, and proportion of the aluminum sheets are harmoniously related to similar qualities in the aluminum beams used in the tower portion of the building. Each curved aluminum sheet suggests varying growth rates and personality types in students. The narrow cylindrical rods which support and join some elements of the sculpture provide a necessary and aesthetically enhancing contrast of shape and size.

LOEB STUDENT CENTER, NEW YORK UNIVERSITY, NEW YORK CITY. *Architect*: Max Abramovitz. *Artist*: Reuben Nakian, abstract sculpture consisting of curved and bent aluminum rectangles, each measuring 6' x 3'; 1961. *Photographer*: Stanley Seligson, New York University.

HUMANITIES BUILDING, WESTERN WASHINGTON STATE COLLEGE, BELLINGHAM, WASHINGTON. *Architects*: Bassetti & Morse. *Artist*: Norman Warsinske, sculptured metal tower, 17' 4"; 1962. *Photographer*: Hugh N. Stratford.

GRADUATE CENTER, HARVARD UNIVERSITY, CAMBRIDGE, MASSACHUSETTS. *Architects*: The Architects Collaborative, Inc. *Partners in Charge*: Walter Gropius, Norman C. Fletcher, Louis A. McMillen, Benjamin Thompson, Robert S. McMillan. *Artist*: Richard Lippold, stainless-steel sculpture, 60' long x 30' high; 1963. *Photographers*: Above—Fiske Photo; Below Left—Fred Stone.

GRADUATE CENTER, HARVARD UNIVERSITY, CAMBRIDGE, MASSACHUSETTS. *Architects*: The Architects Collaborative, Inc. *Partners in Charge*: Walter Gropius, Norman C. Fletcher, Louis A. McMillen, Benjamin Thompson, Robert S. McMillan. *Artist*: Josef Albers, brick chimney; 1949. *Photographer*: Robert Damora.

GRADUATE CENTER, HARVARD UNIVERSITY, CAMBRIDGE, MASSACHUSETTS. *Architects*: The Architects Collaborative, Inc. *Partners in Charge*: Walter Gropius, Norman C. Fletcher, Louis A. McMillen, Benjamin Thompson, Robert S. McMillan. *Artist*: Jean Arp, wood reliefs; 1949. *Photographer*: Fred Stone.

GRADUATE CENTER, HARVARD UNIVERSITY, CAMBRIDGE, MASSACHUSETTS. *Architects*: The Architects Collaborative, Inc. *Partners in Charge*: Walter Gropius, Norman C. Fletcher, Louis A. McMillen, Benjamin Thompson, Robert S. McMillan. *Artist*: Joan Miró, mural; 1963. *Photograph*: Courtesy of Harvard University News Office.

Above and Below:
WOODROW WILSON SCHOOL OF PUBLIC AND INTERNATIONAL AFFAIRS, PRINCETON UNIVERSITY, PRINCETON, NEW JERSEY. *Architect*: Minoru Yamasaki. *Artist*: James Fitzgerald, "Fountain of Freedom," bronze freestanding sculpture, 23' high, weighing approximately 6 tons; 1966. *Photograph*: Courtesy of James Fitzgerald.

LABORATORY THEATER, MOUNT HOLYOKE COLLEGE, SOUTH HADLEY, MASSACHUSETTS. *Architects*: Hugh Stubbins & Associates. *Artist*: Harris Barron, "Dialogue and Movement," precast concrete frieze, 4' 6" high; 1966. *Photographer*: Louis J. Reens.

7

Opposite:
YALE ART AND ARCHITECTURE BUILDING, YALE UNIVERSITY, NEW HAVEN, CONNECTICUT. *Architect*: Paul Rudolph. *Artist*: Robert Engman, concrete tower, 30'; 1963. *Photographer*: Robert Damora.

FACULTY OF PHARMACY, UNIVERSITY OF TORONTO, TORONTO, ONTARIO, CANADA. *Architects*: B. G. Ludlow & Partners. *Artist*: Walter Yarwood, "Cedars," cast bronze sculpture, 7' high x 8' wide x 3½' deep; 1966. *Photographer*: Walter Yarwood.

HAYDEN LIBRARY, MASSACHUSETTS INSTITUTE OF TECHNOLOGY, CAMBRIDGE, MASSACHUSETTS. *Architects*: Voorhees, Walker, Foley & Smith. *Artist*: Dimitri Hadzi, bronze, 6' high; 1963. *Photographer*: MIT Photo.

McDERMOTT COURT, THE GREEN CENTER FOR EARTH SCIENCES, MASSACHUSETTS INSTITUTE OF TECHNOLOGY, CAMBRIDGE, MASSACHUSETTS. *Architects*: I. M. Pei & Associates. *Landscape Architects*: Sasaki, Dawson, DeMay & Associates, Inc. *Artist*: Alexander Calder, "The Big Sail," black steel-plate stabile, weighing 33 tons; 1966. *Photographer*: MIT Photo.

NEW PHYSICS BUILDING, UNIVERSITY OF CALIFORNIA, LOS ANGELES, CALIFORNIA. *Architects:* Neptune & Thomas & Associates. *Artist:* Richard Haines, mosaic and colored-cement mural, eight panels, 12' x 7'; 1962. *Photographer:* Leonora Stevens.

DICKSON ART CENTER, UNIVERSITY OF CALIFORNIA, LOS ANGELES, CALIFORNIA. *Architects:* William L. Pereira & Associates. *Artist:* Jacques Lipchitz, bronze; 1966. *Photographer:* Louis G. Redstone.

LE MOYNE COLLEGE LIBRARY, MEMPHIS, TENNESSEE. *Architects:* Gassner/Nathan/Browne, Inc. *Artist:* Ben Shahn, mural in glass mosaic; 1963. *Photographers:* William W. Carrier, Jr., API Photographers.

MAIN PLAZA, SIMON FRASER UNIVERSITY, BURNABY, BRITISH COLUMBIA, CANADA. *Architects:* Erickson and Massey. *Artist:* Gordon A. Smith, mosaic mural, approximately 12' x 24'; 1966. *Photographer:* Louis G. Redstone.

Above and Below:
LIBRARY, BOWLING GREEN STATE UNIVERSITY, BOWLING GREEN, OHIO. *Architect*: Carl Bentz, head, State Architectural Department of Ohio. *Artists*: Don Drumm Studios, ten-story wall-relief mural, sandblasted concrete, 46' wide x 107' high; 1966. *Photograph*: Courtesy of Bowling Green State University.

CHAPEL, MASSACHUSETTS INSTITUTE OF TECHNOLOGY, CAMBRIDGE, MASSACHUSETTS. *Architects*: Eero Saarinen & Associates; Anderson, Beckwith & Haible. *Artist*: Theodore Roszak, bell tower with aluminum spire, over 30'; 1955. *Photographer*: Balthazar Korab.

WETER MEMORIAL LIBRARY, SEATTLE PACIFIC COLLEGE, SEATTLE, WASHINGTON. *Architect:* Durham, Anderson & Freed. *Artist:* Harold Balazs, fourteen exterior precast mosaic panels, 5' 3" wide x 7' high; theme, historical progression of alphabet design; 1963. *Photographer:* Hugh N. Stratford.

The technique used by the sculptor was to cut out the mold in Styrofoam and then cast. Before the panels were erected, they were sandblasted to achieve a uniform texture.

The panels tell the story of the development of writing through different alphabets. The horizontal diptych of the upper band por-trays Indians carving totems, men painting Egyptian hieroglyphs, scribes writing books in a monastery, and the use of the early printing press. The lower frieze illustrates pictographs, hieroglyphs, early Greek and Roman alphabets, printer's marks, and other symbols of communication.

MUSIC BUILDING, UNIVERSITY OF HAWAII, HONOLULU, HAWAII. *Architect*: Haydn H. Phillips. *Artist*: Murray Turnbull, cast shear panels for structural bends, 7' x 14'; 1962. *Photographer*: James Y. Young.

ORVIS AUDITORIUM, UNIVERSITY OF HAWAII, HONOLULU, HAWAII. *Architect*: Haydn H. Phillips. *Artist*: Edward M. Brownlee, fountain, 4' x 15' 8''; metal mural, 7' x 21'; 1962. *Photographer*: James Y. Young.

UNIVERSITY UNION, FLORIDA STATE UNIVERSITY, TALLAHASSEE, FLORIDA. *Architects*: State University System of Florida; Forrest M. Kelley, Jr., architect to the Florida Board of Regents. *Artists*: Leon Mead and Ralph Hurst, sculptured panels, 9' 4" (above) and 11' 1½" x 44' (below); 1964. *Photographer*: Evon Streetman.

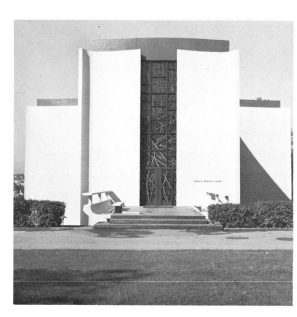

HERRICK MEMORIAL CHAPEL, OCCIDENTAL COLLEGE, LOS ANGELES, CALIFORNIA. *Architects*: Ladd and Kelsey. *Artists*: Malcolm Leland, bronze door pulls, 8' high; Perli Pelzig, stained glass; 1964. *Photograph*: Courtesy of Malcolm Leland.

MEDICAL CENTER, UNIVERSITY OF KENTUCKY, LEXINGTON, KENTUCKY. *Architects*: Ellerbe & Company. *Artist*: Richard Haines, granite inlay and sandblast mural, 16' high x 80' long; 1958. *Photographer*: Leonora Stevens.

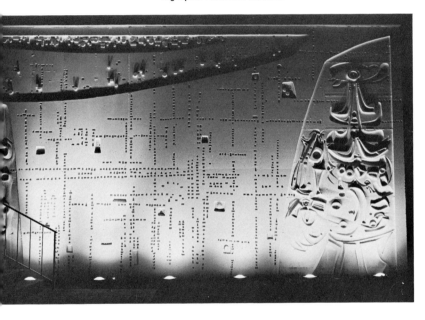

RUSSELL OLT STUDENT CENTER, ANDERSON COLLEGE, ANDERSON, INDIANA. *Architects*: Johnson, Ritchart and Associates. *Artist*: Robert Youngman, precast concrete panels, 18' x 20' x 18''; 1964. *Photographer*: Robert Youngman.

RESEARCH LIBRARY, UNIVERSITY OF CALIFORNIA, LOS ANGELES, CALIFORNIA. *Architects*: Jones and Emmons. *Artist*: David Smith, metal sculpture; 1964. *Photographer*: Julius Shulman.

Just as art is becoming a part of the university student's campus environment, so, on a smaller scale, the elementary or secondary school may provide exciting experiences outside classes. The art may take the form of colorful murals executed in colored glazed brick as an integral part of the masonry wall or of ceramic and mosaic murals. It may also take the form of precast concrete bas-reliefs and outdoor concrete play sculpture, which the children enjoy. The reaction of a ten-year-old child to a colorful mural in a new school was: "Everything is so wonderful, but the mural is the prettiest. I just keep looking and looking!" This reaction expresses the innate thirst of youth for stimulating sensory experiences—color, imagery, texture, and design. Often, such experiences can be the inspiration for talented children to express their own ideas in art.

The problem of budgeting for art in schools is a difficult one. However, if the architect plans the art program in his original budget in the form of allowances for special materials and "special labor," then everything becomes a part of the building costs. The end result invariably is greeted with pleasant reactions from all—students, parents, and teachers.

JULIAN H. KROLIK ELEMENTARY SCHOOL, DETROIT, MICHIGAN, *Architects*: Louis G. Redstone Associates, Inc. *Artist*: Arthur Schneider, concrete play sculpture, 5' high; 1962. *Photographers*: Lens-Art Studio.

INDIAN HILLS HIGH SCHOOL, CINCINNATI, OHIO. *Architect*: Woodward Garber. *Artist*: Robert Youngman, cast-in-place concrete, entry-court garden, main slab, 67' x 5½' x 18''; 1966. *Photographer*: Norman Cook Studios.

IRVING ELEMENTARY SCHOOL, EUGENE, OREGON. *Architects*: Morin & Longwood. *Artist*: Harold Balazs, sculptured panels, 4' x 11'; 1966. *Photographer*: Hugh N. Stratford.

WYLIE E. GROVES HIGH SCHOOL, BIRMINGHAM, MICHIGAN. *Architects*: Smith, Demiene, Kasprzak, Adams, Inc. *Artist*: Architects' staff, colored-tile mural wall, 40' x 5'; 1960. *Photographers*: Lens-Art Studio.

BERRY ELEMENTARY SCHOOL, DETROIT, MICHIGAN. *Architects*: Louis G. Redstone Associates, Inc. *Artist*: Richard Jennings, glazed-brick mural, 30' x 10'; 1962. *Photographer*: Allen Stross.

INTERIOR COURT, GLAZER ELEMENTARY SCHOOL, DETROIT, MICHIGAN. *Architects*: Louis G. Red-stone Associates, Inc. *Artist*: Narendra Patel, "Festival," glazed-brick mural, 20' x 12'; 1966. *Photog-rapher*: Daniel Bartush.

WEST BRIDGEWATER ELEMENTARY SCHOOL, WEST BRIDGEWATER, MASSACHUSETTS. *Architects*: The Architects Collaborative, Inc. *Artist*: Herbert Bayer, colored-tile mural; 1956. *Photographers*: Rob-ert D. Harvey Studio.

EAST VALLEY HIGH SCHOOL, SPOKANE, WASHINGTON.
Architect: Kenneth W. Brooks. *Artist*: Harold Balazs, "Three Knights," sculpture of welded steel, 5' and 10' high; 1961. *Photographer*: Charles Pearson.

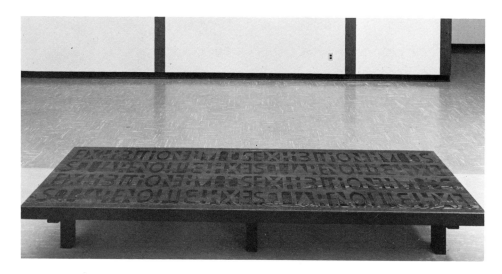

EAST VALLEY HIGH SCHOOL, SPOKANE, WASHINGTON.
Architect: Kenneth W. Brooks. *Artist*: Harold Balazs, benches made of fir, 2' 6" wide x 10' long x 1' 4" high; 1961. *Photographer*: Charles Pearson.

In looking toward the future, we should develop a nucleus of upcoming artists and architects who think in terms of collaboration between the professions. It is good to see that steps are now being taken to foster this idea.

A worthwhile stimulus in creating interest among senior high school students in art appreciation and in the understanding of urban design problems is the use of city-wide competitions for the design of neighborhood units or other public buildings. These competitions could require the inclusion of art as part of the overall design. The fact that the students have no special training in this field may bring out fresh ideas, even though there may not be immediate practical application. The main benefit is that the students themselves get a deeper understanding of ways to judge their surroundings. Another possibility to consider for student encouragement is the granting of yearly awards to outstanding would-be architectural students using art in their designs.

To summarize, school environment enhanced by art and periodic competitions to stimulate the students' interest in art should produce more receptive and understanding individuals.

KINDERGARTEN, PUBLIC SCHOOL NO. 18, BRONX, NEW YORK. *Architects*: O'Connor & Kilham. *Artist*: Joseph Kiselewski, "Bull Frog," polished green granite at entrance, 3'; 1951. *Photograph*: Courtesy of Joseph Kiselewski.

CAPT. ARTHUR ROTH ELEMENTARY SCHOOL, CLEVELAND, OHIO. *Architects*: Madison, Madison & Madison. *Artist*: William M. McVey, cast aluminum and chrome-plated sculpture with glazed stoneware, 22' x 26'; 1965. *Photograph*: Courtesy of William M. McVey.

MUSEUMS AND LIBRARIES

The new concept of museum planning aims at a smaller building in relation to the site. As a result, the landscape areas surrounding the building are larger and permit a greater integration of the arts as part of the overall planning. The exterior of the museum is adaptable for permanent works of art in a setting which becomes a part of the landscape and is related to the entire design concept. This new museum image stresses the idea that art does not have to be confined to gallery exhibits. Permanent pieces of art, such as monumental sculpture, fountains, and especially designed landscape gardens, create a stimulating mood even before the visitor enters the museum building.

Although library buildings have a different function to perform, they also can serve as a stimulus for art awareness. More persons of all ages use library facilities, and for many of them works of art as part of the building concept are their first experience with art. In branch libraries, small interior courtyards which can be viewed from several directions are good locations for freestanding sculpture, fountains, or wall murals.

Main library buildings can use art on a larger scale. Here, interior and exterior murals, expressing historical events or abstract symbolic forms, can be incorporated in the building design. If funds are available and the site is ample, fountains and freestanding sculpture can add to the enhancement of the surroundings.

Both museums and libraries serve as excellent starting places to open new vistas in art discovery for the visitor.

A good example of procedure in developing an art program for a library building project is that used for the Salt Lake City Public Library. Right from the outset, the architects and the library board set up a budget to include works of art. An advisory committee under the board consisted of the architect, the dean of the Fine Arts School at the University of Utah, the director of the Salt Lake Art Center, and the Fine Arts librarian. The committee was charged with making recommendations, selections, and contractual arrangements for artists. The results have been very gratifying.

LOS ANGELES COUNTY MUSEUM OF ART, LOS AN-
GELES, CALIFORNIA. *Architects*: William L. Pereira &
Associates. *Artist*: Sorel Etrog, "Moses," bronze sculp-
ture; 1964. *Photographer*: Museum staff photographer.

LOS ANGELES COUNTY MUSEUM OF ART, LOS ANGELES, CALIFORNIA. *Architects*: William L.
Pereira & Associates. *Artist*: Alexander Calder, mobile sculpture; 1964. *Photographer*: Balthazar Korab.

WEST WING ADDITION, SAN DIEGO FINE ARTS GALLERY, SAN DIEGO, CALIFORNIA. *Architects*: Mosher & Drew. *Artist*: Malcolm Leland, grillwork, gates, bronze-anodized cast aluminum, 3' x 8' high (technique developed under Graham Foundation grant for advanced studies in fine arts); 1966. *Photographer*: Malcolm Leland.

HAWAII MEDICAL LIBRARY, HONOLULU, HAWAII. *Architects*: Vladimir Ossipoff & Associates. *Artist*: Edward M. Brownlee, "Flames of Prometheus," metal sculpture, 9' 6" on pedestal 18" off deck; 1964. *Photographer*: David Cornwell.

SEATTLE PUBLIC LIBRARY, SEATTLE, WASHINGTON. *Architects*: Bindon & Wright; associates, Decker, Christenson & Kitchin. *Artist*: George Tsutakawa, "Fountain of Wisdom," bronze fountain sculpture, 15' high; 1960. *Photographer*: Hal Porter.

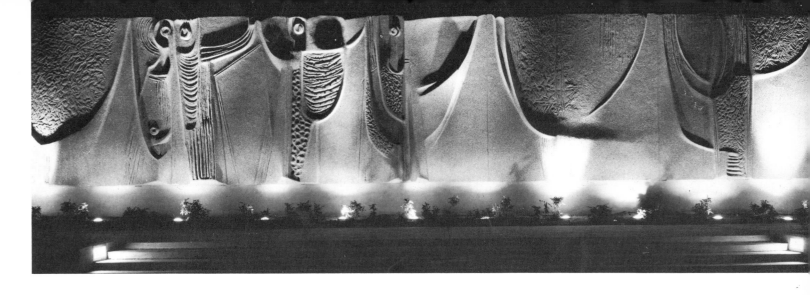

SALT LAKE CITY PUBLIC LIBRARY, SALT LAKE CITY, UTAH. *Architects*: Edwards & Daniels. *Artist*: Jo Roper, cast stone bas-relief, 52' x 10'; 1964. *Photographer*: Ed Hunt. Below: At night.

WASHINGTON STATE LIBRARY, OLYMPIA, WASHINGTON. *Architect*: Paul Thiry. *Artist*: James Fitzgerald, marble mosaic wall, 16' x 22'; 1959. *Photograph*: Courtesy of Paul Thiry.

25

INTERIOR COURT, WILDER BRANCH, DETROIT PUBLIC LIBRARY, DETROIT, MICHIGAN. *Architects*: Louis G. Redstone Associates, Inc. *Artist*: Narendra Patel, mural of fused metals on copper; largest element, 7' x 4'; 1966. *Photographer*: Daniel Bartush.

COSSITT LIBRARY, MEMPHIS, TENNESSEE. *Architects*: Walk Jones/Mah & Jones/ Architects, Inc. *Artist*: Edwin C. Rust, "The Teacher," freestanding sculpture; 1959. *Photographers*: API Photographers.

WILMOT BRANCH LIBRARY, TUCSON, ARIZONA. *Architects*: Nicholas Sakellar & Associates. *Artist*: James Savage, carvings in cast concrete blocks, recording of man's progress in knowledge and writing; 1965. *Photographers*: Manley Commercial Photography.

Opposite:
LOS ANGELES COUNTY MUSEUM OF ART, LOS ANGELES, CALIFORNIA. *Architects*: William L. Pereira & Associates. *Artist*: Norbert Krickey; 1964. *Photographer*: Julius Shulman.

METROPOLITAN OPERA HOUSE, LINCOLN CENTER FOR THE PERFORMING ARTS, NEW YORK CITY. *Architects*: Harrison & Abramovitz. *Artist*: Marc Chagall, "Triumph of Music," mural, 30' x 36'; 1966. *Photographers*: Sylvania Electric Products, Inc.; Joseph Costa.

In New York City, where over half a million visitors come to enjoy a rich variety of cultural events in opera, theater, music, and dance, the dramatic effect of the architecture and the integrated plastic arts of Lincoln Center serves as an added aesthetic experience.

The general plan is that of a group of rectangular buildings, which includes the Metropolitan Opera House, flanked on the south by the New York State Theater and on the north by Philharmonic Hall.

Artist: Marc Chagall, "Triumph of Music," in south lobby.

PUBLIC AND CIVIC BUILDINGS

This book stresses a point of view that art should reach every citizen in every walk of life. There could not be more appropriate places to afford people the pleasure of experiencing art than our public and civic buildings. The large auditoriums where thousands congregate and spend many hours, the airports where the visitor gets his first reaction and forms his image of the new city and where the departing traveler spends his waiting time enjoying the stimulating effect that art can evoke, the theaters and symphony halls where people come primarily to enjoy cultural events and where the fine arts are a natural element in the total "climate," the city halls where citizens from all income groups, at one time or another, come on personal business and where exposure to the fine arts is often their first and only experience—all these public places present a great opportunity to develop awareness among large numbers of people.

The examples in the following pages show the variety of art forms and art media which can be used in connection with architectural elements. Some of these buildings were financed through private fund raising, endowments, and bequests. However, most of the civic buildings were financed in part by city, state, and Federal funds. There is every reason to follow the example of the Federal government in allocating from 1/2 percent to 1 percent of the construction budget to art. Now is the time for us all to make every effort to see that our legislators approve such measures. Almost every metropolitan area is in the throes of planning or building a cultural and recreational center complex in its inner-city renewal area. We must not miss this opportunity to bring the added meaning which the human touch of the artist provides.

An outstanding achievement in attaining artistic synthesis was reached in the planning of the Toronto International Airport for the Canadian Department of Transport. Under the formula of allocating a sum of up to 1/2 percent of construction costs for fine arts, a budget of up to $160,000 was provided for murals and sculptures.

In planning the overall art needs, an advisory panel on fine arts to the government of Canada was consulted. The panel included the director of the National Gallery of Canada, the director of the Montreal Museum of Fine Arts, the directors of the schools of architecture of Winnipeg and Toronto, the director of the Art Gallery of Toronto, and representatives of the architectural firm which planned the airport.

The art work is so planned that the first impact is from the exterior, in the large plaza of the administration building. Here the art of Eskimo origin—"The Inussuks [pronounced Inuk-suks]"—is shown. This art consists of tall stone figures assembled by Eskimos for use as markers and beacons for travelers and explorers in the Arctic regions.

Toronto's Inussuks were the first to be brought from the north. During the summer of 1962 the Eskimos of Cape Dorset on Baffin Island made three replicas of the ancient beacons. Each rock was numbered; the stone figures were photographed from several angles, then taken down and transported in empty fuel-oil barrels by a Canadian Coast Guard vessel. With the aid of the numbered rocks and photographs, reassemblage at the airport was relatively easy. The Inussuks were mounted on concrete plinths, and a plaque was added to explain their significance.

Within the building, at the east and west ends of the main concourse, are two open courtyards. The circular "ring" concourse which leads passengers to their aircraft encloses the courts on the outside. Sculptures by two Montreal artists, Armand Vaillancourt and Louis Archambault, are in the east and west courts, respectively.

Great attention was given to color and texture effects in the departure rooms. The use of twelve ceramic walls, each of different colors in a graded sequence of red, orange, yellow, green, blue, and violet, gives a sense of immediate identity with a single area. These walls, 25 feet wide and 13 feet high, were designed by Claude Vermette.

In summary, the successful integration of art in total planning is due primarily to the decision to include the art work right from the beginning, to the allocation of an adequate budget, and to the use of professional advisers to commission competent artists.

This procedure is basic to achieve best results.

TORONTO INTERNATIONAL AIRPORT, MALTON, ONTARIO, CANADA. *Architects*: John B. Parkin Associates. *Artists*: "Innusuks," primitive Eskimo carvings, 7' and 8' high; 1964. *Photographers*: Panda Associates Photography.

TORONTO INTERNATIONAL AIRPORT, MALTON, ONTARIO, CANADA. *Architects*: John B. Parkin Associates. *Artist*: Harold Town, perforated and sculptured brass screen, 8' x 20', weighing over 1,000 pounds; 1964. *Photographers*: Panda Associates Photography.

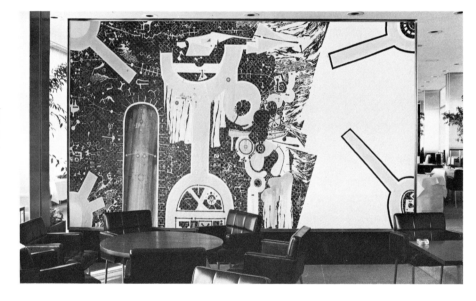

TORONTO INTERNATIONAL AIRPORT, MALTON, ONTARIO, CANADA. *Architects*: John B. Parkin Associates. *Artist*: Louis De Niverville, mural, 9' x 16'; 1964. *Photographers*: Panda Associates Photography.

TORONTO INTERNATIONAL AIRPORT, MALTON, ONTARIO, CANADA. *Architects*: John B. Parkin Associates. *Artist*: Louis Archambault, "Levitation," steel sculpture, 30' 6" high; 1964. *Photographers*: Panda Associates Photography.

LOBBY, PLACE DES ARTS, MONTREAL, CANADA. *Architects*: Affleck, Desbarats, Dimakopoulos, Lebensold, Sise. *Artist*: Louis Archambault, "Three Radiant Angels," welded Muntz bronze sheets, 60' long x 12' high; 1963. *Photographers*: Panda Associates Photography.

TORONTO CITY HALL, TORONTO, CANADA. *Architects*: Viljo Revell; John B. Parkin Associates. *Artist*: Henry Moore, "The Archer," bronze, 10' 8" high x 7' 4" wide x 11' 2" long; 1966. *Photographers*: Left, Panda Associates Photography; below, George Zonars; right, Joseph Messana.

SEATTLE CENTER COLISEUM, SEATTLE, WASHINGTON. *Architect*: Paul Thiry. *Artist*: Everett Dupen, cast bronze sculptured fountain, 20' high; horizontal modeling in basin, terrazzo over concrete; pool, 80' x 120'; 1962. *Photograph*: Courtesy of Paul Thiry.

LOBBY, ADMINISTRATION BUILDING, CENTRAL DISTRICT WATER FILTRATION PLANT, CHICAGO, ILLINOIS. *Architects*: C. F. Murphy Associates. *Artist*: Milton Horn, "Hymn to Water," bronze relief sculpture, 10' x 24' 4½"; 1966. *Photographer*: Estelle Horn.

In this bronze relief the structural design, character and spirit developed simultaneously. Each created form, whether evoking a creative force, a human, animal, fish, fowl, plant, planet or water image, developed its place of being in this sculpture, its shape, its varying relief projections and its size in the organism of the whole. Sometimes it was the shape that came first and drew to itself symbolic meaning. Sometimes it was nature's forms that suggested the right sculptural form, treatment and symbol. But whether we read these as symbol, "abstract" or "representational" forms they interact in the life of the whole work and the whole interacts with the scale of the room and the people in the room.

Milton Horn

FONTANA CITY HALL, FONTANA, CALIFORNIA. *Architect*: Grover W. Taylor. *Artist*: François Stahly, steel fountain, 38' high; 1962. *Photographers*: Kaiser Graphic Arts.

THE CHICAGO CIVIC CENTER, CHICAGO, ILLINOIS. *Architects*: C. F. Murphy Associates; Skidmore, Owings & Merrill; and Loebl Schlossman Bennett & Dart. *Artist*: Pablo Picasso, steel sculpture, 50' high; 1967. *Photographers*: Ezra Stoller Associates.

LOBBY, WHITING AUDITORIUM, FLINT, MICHIGAN. *Architects*: Smith, Hinchman & Grylls Associates, Inc. *Artist*: Harry Bertoia, bronzed steel, 7' in diameter; 1967. *Photographer*: Bob Wallace.

THEATER, FRESNO CONVENTION CENTER, FRESNO, CALIFORNIA.
Architects: Adrian Wilson & Associates; Robert Stevens Associates.
Artist: Stanley C. Bitters, cast bronze doors, 12' x 25'; 1966. *Photographer*: Gayle Smalley.

EUGENE CITY HALL, EUGENE, OREGON. *Architects*: Morin & Longwood. *Artist*: Jan Zach, wood sculpture (above), 16' long and 4' in diameter; metal sculpture (below), 8' high; 1964. *Photographer*: Hugh N. Stratford.

CIVIC AUDITORIUM, JACKSONVILLE, FLORIDA. *Architects*: Kemp, Bunch & Jackson. *Artist*: Roy Craven, sand-sculpture mural, 17' x 33'; free-form design representing the "many moods of the community"; 1962. *Photographers*: Bodden Fotos.

NEW YORK STATE THEATER, LINCOLN CENTER FOR THE PERFORMING ARTS, NEW YORK CITY. *Architects*: Philip Johnson Associates. *Artist*: Philip Johnson, bronze fountain, 168' x 260', 32' in diameter; 1964. *Photographers*: Ezra Stoller Associates.

LINCOLN CENTER FOR THE PERFORMING ARTS, NEW YORK CITY. *Architects*: Harrison & Abramovitz. *Artist*: Henry Moore, "A Leg Part and a Head & Arms Part," 16' x 30'; 1965. *Photographer*: O. E. Nelson.

VIVIAN BEAUMONT THEATER, LINCOLN CENTER FOR THE PERFORMING ARTS, NEW YORK CITY. *Architects*: Eero Saarinen & Associates. *Artist*: Henry Moore, monumental bronze sculpture, which stands in reflecting pool (to the left is plaza entrance to library and museum), 16' by 30'; 1965. *Photographer*: David Hirsch.

PHILHARMONIC HALL, LINCOLN CENTER FOR THE PERFORMING ARTS, NEW YORK CITY. *Architects*: Harrison & Abramovitz. *Artist*: Richard Lippold, "Orpheus and Apollo," sculpture consisting of 190 sheets of Muntz metal and stainless-steel cables, placed in grand promenade, 190' long; 1962. *Photographer*: Bob Serating.

Magnificently modern, light and airy sculpture relating in a contemporary manner to the interior of the foyer under special lighting, sparkles and reflects rays of light to delight the eye.

Max Abramovitz, architect of Philharmonic Hall

Opposite:
PHILHARMONIC HALL, LINCOLN CEN-
TER FOR THE PERFORMING ARTS, NEW
YORK CITY. *Architects*: Harrison &
Abramovitz. *Artist*: Seymour Lipton, "Arch-
angel," bronze and Monel metal sculpture,
9' high x 8' wide, placed on plaza level
of Philharmonic Hall; 1964. *Photograph*:
Courtesy of Lincoln Center for the Per-
forming Arts.

LINCOLN CENTER FOR THE PERFORMING ARTS, NEW YORK
CITY. *Architects*: Skidmore, Owings & Merrill. *Artist*: Alexander
Calder, "Le Guichet" (ticket window), blackened steel stabile, placed
at approaches to the Library and Museum of the Performing Arts,
22' x 14', weighing 3,000 pounds; 1964. *Photograph*: Courtesy of
Lincoln Center for the Performing Arts.

PHILHARMONIC HALL, LINCOLN CENTER FOR THE PERFORMING
ARTS, NEW YORK CITY. *Architects*: Harrison & Abramovitz. *Artist*:
Dimitri Hadzi, "K.458, The Hunt," sculpture derived from Mozart's
string quartet, cast in bronze, 10½' high; 1964. *Photographer*: Bob
Serating.

COURTYARD, SEATTLE CENTER PLAYHOUSE, SEATTLE, WASH-INGTON. *Architects*: Kirk, Wallace, McKinley & Associates. *Artist*: James Fitzgerald, "Fountain of the Northwest," 18' high, weighing 6,000 pounds; 1962. *Photographer*: Hugh N. Stratford.

This sculpture represents an attempt to continue and to complete, in a sense, the gesture begun by a beautifully conceived architectural space. This gesture is the result of two related, but untouching elements, appearing first in the walls of the Lobby, where it establishes the main space of that area of the building, and reappearing again and again in the smallest details of the design. The result is a constant opening of space between the curving, sympathetic elements. . . .

The dimensions of the two forms relate both to human scale and to established dimensions of the architecture, so that the sculpture acts as a liaison between the grandeur of the architectural scale and the scale of the spectator. This rapport is furthered by the gesture of the sculpture as it completes the invitation begun by the architecture.

Richard Lippold

JONES HALL FOR THE PERFORMING ARTS, HOUSTON, TEXAS. *Architects*: Caudill, Rowlett & Scott. *Artist*: Richard Lippold, "Gemini II," two sculptural forms consisting of 90,000' of gold-plated stainless-steel wire, fastening 2,300 aluminum rods; 1966. *Photographers*: Bert Brandt & Associates.

METROPOLITAN OPERA HOUSE, LINCOLN CENTER FOR THE PERFORMING ARTS, NEW YORK CITY. *Architects*: Harrison & Abramovitz. *Artist*: Marc Chagall, "Source of Music," mural, 30' x 36'; 1966. *Photographers*: Sylvania Electric Products, Inc.; Joseph Costa.

Lincoln Center Plaza is a public area which embraces the Lincoln Center fountain, as well as a northern part containing a reflecting pool. Facing the reflecting pool is the Vivian Beaumont Theater. Also in this area is the Forum, a smaller theater, and the Library and Museum of the Performing Arts. The Juilliard building is linked to this northern part of Lincoln Center Plaza by a terrace-bridge spanning Sixty-fifth Street.

It is exciting and heartening to see the variety of approaches of media, subject, and style of the excellent sculptural pieces of murals which form part of the architectural complex: the strong mood created, day or night, by the monumental bronze sculpture of Henry Moore in the reflecting pool of Lincoln Center Plaza North; the striking effect made by Alexander Calder's "Le Guichet," Richard Lippold's monumental space sculpture "Orpheus and Apollo," Dimitri Hadzi's "The Hunt," and Seymour Lipton's "Archangel"; the dynamic expression of Jacques Lipchitz's bronze relief; the appealing murals by Marc Chagall; the bas-relief murals by Lee Bontecou and Dufy; and other excellent works of artists which are not presented in this book. These include sculptures by Edward Higgins, Jasper Johns, Reuben Nakian, Francesco Somaini, and Elie Nadelman.

OUR LADY OF THE ANGELS SEMINARY OF THE FATHERS OF THE CONGREGATION OF THE MISSION OF ST. VINCENT DE PAUL, ALBANY, NEW YORK. *Architects*: Max O. Urbahn. *Artist*: Jean Barillet, east window, triangular shape, 54' wide x 50' high; theme, "Our Lady of the Angels"; 1963. *Photographer*: Ezra Stoller Associates.

AIR FORCE ACADEMY CADET CHAPEL, COLORADO SPRINGS, COLORADO. *Architects*: Skidmore, Owings & Merrill. *Artists*: Judson Studios and Walter Netsch of Skidmore, Owings & Merrill, stained-glass windows; 1963. *Photographers*: Stewarts Commercial Photographers, Inc. *Photograph*: Courtesy of USAF Academy Photo.

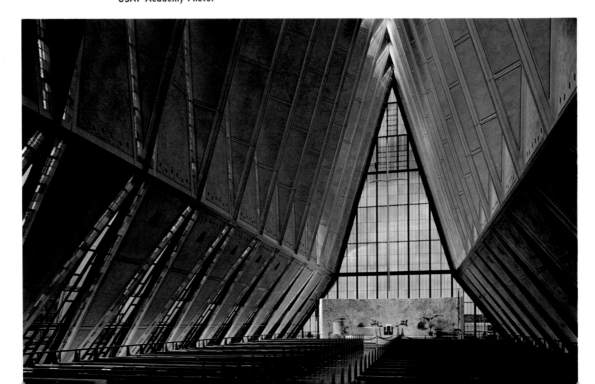

RELIGIOUS BUILDINGS

The postwar decades have witnessed revolutionary changes in the acceptance of new architectural and art forms by most of the religious groups.

Many factors have contributed to these changes. The increasing tendency of religious institutions to become centers of communal and educational activities has been one important factor. Another factor has been the growing interest in all art forms on the part of both the clergy and members of the general public who realize the spiritual and inspirational value of art. Art gives a building a character of its own and adds a unique quality. The awakening interest in art is also confirmed by the churches' sponsorship of numerous art exhibitions in their community halls and by the great public interest in the national religious art shows. In the National Religious Art Exhibition held at the Cranbrook Academy of Art in 1966, the artists' approach to religious themes varied from conservative representational forms to out-and-out abstractions in every type of media.

The new materials and techniques of construction have led many Catholic and Protestant churches and synagogues to use new forms in architecture and art. The art forms created from a variety of new materials, such as stainless steel, welded metals, acrylic paints, concrete, and plastics, give a tremendous impact to the interiors of the churches and synagogues and express the radical changes that are taking place in the religious life of the country.

Although art has always played an important role in church architecture, it is only in the past few decades that synagogues have reinterpreted the Biblical commandment not to make graven images. Art in synagogues today expresses the varied contemporary approaches by using Biblical themes and present-day events in Jewish life, as well as the religious ideals of brotherhood.

I have included several examples of religious structures which have in themselves a sculptural quality. Often, art in these cases would only detract from the total concept.

In the section dealing with the United Nations headquarters, the importance of art is emphasized as a dynamic force in providing a common interest, understanding, and tolerance among all the nations of the world. The same dynamics of art forms could be applied at home at the grass-roots level in the religious activities of all denominations, large or small. Here art expressions may well become the common denominator for better relationships and understanding among persons of different faiths.

TEMPLE OHEB SHALOM, BALTIMORE, MARY-
LAND. *Architects*: The Architects Collaborative,
Inc. *Partner in Charge*: Walter Gropius, with
Leavitt Associates. *Artist*: Gyorgy Kepes, ark;
1961. *Photographers*: Joseph W. Molitor Photog-
raphy.

TEMPLE OHEB SHALOM, BALTIMORE, MARY-
LAND. *Architects*: The Architects Collaborative,
Inc. *Partner in Charge*: Walter Gropius, with
Leavitt Associates. *Artist*: Gyorgy Kepes, menorah;
1961. *Photograph*: Courtesy of the Architects
Collaborative, Inc.

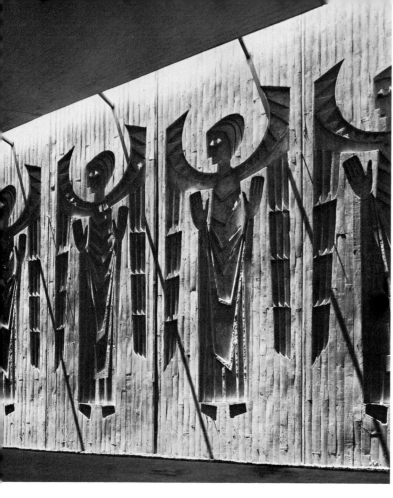

ST. PATRICK'S CHURCH, OKLAHOMA CITY, OKLAHOMA. *Architects*: Murray Jones Murray. *Artist*: Josef Albers, dossal screen, 16' x 28'; 1962. *Photographer*: Ben Newby.

ST. PATRICK'S CHURCH, OKLAHOMA CITY, OKLAHOMA. *Architects*: Murray Jones Murray. *Artist*: Frank Kacmarcik, sculptured concrete panels, 10' x 30'; 1962. *Photographer*: Julius Shulman.

ST. PATRICK'S CHURCH, OKLAHOMA CITY, OKLAHOMA. *Achitects*: Murray Jones Murray. *Artist*: Ludwig Schermer, stained glass; 1962. *Photographer*: Ben Newby.

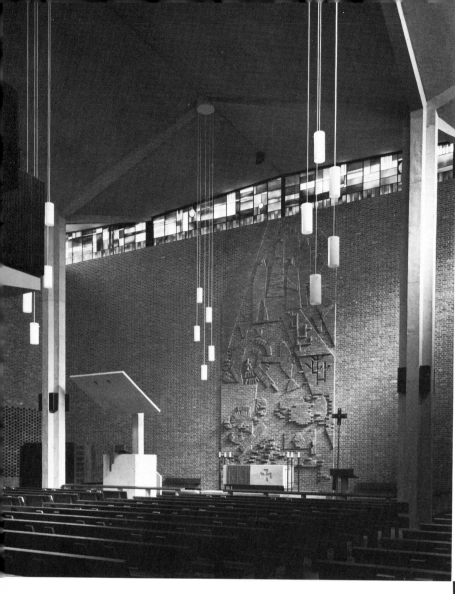

FIRST LUTHERAN CHURCH, ST. PETER, MINNESOTA. *Architects*: Harold Spitznagel & Associates. *Artist*: Robert Aldern, brick mural; 1965. *Photographer*: Joel Strasser.

CHRIST THE VICTOR CHAPEL, FIRST LUTHERAN CHURCH, SIOUX FALLS, SOUTH DAKOTA. *Architects*: Harold Spitznagel & Associates. *Artists*: Palmer Eide, metal sculpture and sand castings; Emil Frei, leaded glass windows; 1965. *Photographer*: Joel Strasser.

SHAAREY ZEDEK SYNAGOGUE, SOUTHFIELD, MICHIGAN. *Architect*: Percival Goodman. *Associate Architects*: Albert Kahn Associated Architects & Engineers, Inc. *Artists*: Jan Peter Stern, "Tree of Life," stainless steel, 36' high; Robert Pinart, stained-glass windows; 1962. *Photographers*: Benyas-Kaufman.

CHICAGO LOOP SYNAGOGUE, CHICAGO, ILLINOIS. *Architects*: Loebl Schlossman Bennett & Dart. *Artist*: Abraham Rattner, stained-glass window, executed by Jean Barillet; 1960. *Photographer*: Joseph P. Messana.

UNITED CHURCH OF ROWAYTON, ROWAYTON, CONNECTICUT. *Architect*: Joseph Salerno; 1962. *Photographer*: Joseph P. Messana.

ST. JOHN'S ABBEY, COLLEGEVILLE, MINNESOTA. *Architects*: Marcel Breuer and Associates; 1960. *Photographer*: Joseph P. Messana.

Below and Right:
FIRST PRESBYTERIAN CHURCH, STAMFORD, CONNECTICUT. *Architects*: Harrison & Abramovitz; Sherwood, Mills & Smith. *Artist*: Gabriel Loire, stained-glass windows; 1963. *Photographer*: Joseph P. Messana.

Above:
NORTH CHRISTIAN CHURCH, COLUMBUS, INDIANA. *Architects*: Eero Saarinen & Associates; 1964. *Photographer*: Joseph P. Messana.

Right:
GREEK ORTHODOX CHURCH OF THE ANNUNCIATION, MILWAUKEE, WISCONSIN. *Architect*: Frank Lloyd Wright; 1961. *Photographer*: Joseph P. Messana.

ROOFLESS CHURCH, NEW HARMONY, INDIANA. *Architects*: Philip Johnson Associates. *Artist*: Jacques Lipchitz, gates; 1960. *Photographer*: James K. Mellow.

ROOFLESS CHURCH, NEW HARMONY, INDIANA. *Architects*: Philip Johnson Associates. *Artist*: Jacques Lipchitz, sculptured Madonna; 1960. *Photographer*: James K. Mellow.

SHRINE OF OUR LADY OF THE SNOWS, BELLEVILLE, ILLINOIS. *Architect*: Richard Cummings; 1962. *Landscape Architect*: Emmett Layton. *Photograph*: Courtesy of Shrine of Our Lady of the Snows.

SHRINE OF OUR LADY OF THE SNOWS, BELLEVILLE, ILLINOIS. *Architect*: Richard Cummings. *Landscape Architect*: Emmett Layton. *Artist*: William Severson, Byzantine turrets over bells (tuned to D, F, G, and B flat), cast in Germany; 1963. *Photograph*: Courtesy of Shrine of Our Lady of the Snows.

TEMPLE SINAI, WASHINGTON, D.C. *Architects*: Nicholas Satterlee & Associates. *Artist*: Boris Aronson, ark, menorah, lectern; 1961. *Photographer*: Robert C. Lautman.

FRIDLEY CHURCH, FRIDLEY, MINNESOTA. *Architects*: Harold Spitznagel & Associates. *Artists*: Peter Eide and Palmer Eide, "Cloud," composed of plywood panels covered with burlap over which paint and sand have been applied, 36' long x 15' wide; 1966. *Photographers*: Warren Reynolds & Associates.

TEMPLE BETH AM, LOS ANGELES, CALIFORNIA. *Architect*: Mathew Lapota. *Artist*: Perli Pelzig, "The Wall of the Martyred Six Million"; 1966. *Photographer*: Julius Shulman.

MOUNT SINAI TEMPLE, EL PASO, TEXAS. *Architects*: Sidney Eisenshtat & Associates. *Associate Architects*: Carroll & Dauble. *Artists*: Ted Egri, bronze ark doors; Jacques Duval, faceted glass; 1965. *Photographer*: Julius Shulman.

WESLEY FOUNDATION CHAPEL, MEMPHIS STATE UNIVERSITY, MEMPHIS, TENNESSEE. *Architects*: Dean E. Hill & Associates. *Artist*: Bob Galanti, "Crown of Thorns"; 1959. *Photograph*: Courtesy of Dean E. Hill & Associates.

SAN MARINO CONGREGATIONAL CHURCH, SAN MARINO, CALIFORNIA. *Architects*: Smith, Powell & Morgridge. *Artist*: Tom Van Sant, "Tree of Life," mural in natural stone set in epoxy resin and silica sand, 30' high x 15' wide; 1960. *Photographer*: Larry Frost. *Photograph*: Courtesy of Powell, Morgridge, Richards and Coghlan.

MIDLAND FIRST METHODIST CHURCH, MIDLAND, MICHIGAN. *Architects*: Alden B. Dow Associates, Inc. *Artist*: Alden B. Dow, gate; added 1954. *Photographer*: Gerald Gard.

OAK PARK TEMPLE, OAK PARK, ILLINOIS. *Architects*: Walter H. Sobel & Associates. *Artists*: A. Raymond Katz, ark doors and perpetual light; Rodney M. Winfield and Emil Frei, two chapel stained-glass windows, each 5' x 30'; 1955. *Photographers*: Bill Engdahl, Hedrich-Blessing.

TEMPLE ISRAEL, ST. LOUIS, MISSOURI. *Architects*: Helmuth, Obata & Kassabaum. *Artist*: Rodney M. Winfield, tabernacle, lectern, podium, chairs, of bronze, steel, and wood; 1962. *Photographers*: Hedrich-Blessing.

SHOPPING CENTERS

One of the basic goals of a shopping center is to develop a festive and colorful environment, to create a marketplace that makes shopping a gayer, more interesting experience set in attractive surroundings. This concept holds true for both open- and closed-mall centers. To carry out the concept, the architect has to be especially aware of the proportions, scale, and character of the malls and sheltered crosswalks (in open malls). The use of related art, i.e., murals, sculpture, planting, fountains, paving design, special lighting, and graphics, adds a human touch and meaningful interest. The fact that many people visit shopping centers for browsing as well as for shopping, even on Sundays when stores are closed, proves the validity of the concept. There is no doubt that a well-programmed use of art could create a special regional atmosphere which would make a center a landmark. However, a word of caution is in order here. Indiscriminate or misdirected use of art could result in an undesirable "image" and could do more harm than good. In any case, an art program, with the advice of the architect in charge and of a knowledgeable art consultant, is a prerequisite.

While the reasons for the use of art in an enclosed shopping center are similar to those for its use in an open-mall center, the type and arrangement of art pose different problems for the artist and the architect. The enclosed-mall center, by its very nature, is more intimate in character, and the works of art have to be more precisely scaled to its interior spaces (in very much the same way as an interior arrangement in a house). The artist has a greater choice of materials, inasmuch as the art pieces are protected from the weather and are under a constant temperature.

WESTLAND CENTER, WESTLAND, MICHIGAN. *Architects*: Victor Gruen Associates; Louis G. Redstone Associates, Inc. *Artist*: George Rickey, freestanding steel sculpture, 30'; 1965. *Photographer*: Balthazar Korab. Below: *Artist*: Earl Krentzin, metal sculpture, 10'; 1965.

GENERAL VIEW OF EAST COURT, WESTLAND CENTER, WESTLAND, MICHIGAN. *Architects:* Victor Gruen Associates; Louis G. Redstone Associates, Inc.; 1965. *Photographer:* Balthazar Korab.

NORTHLAND CENTER, SOUTHFIELD, MICHIGAN. *Architects:* Victor Gruen Associates. *Artist:* Richard Jennings, metal fountain, 15' x 20'; 1954. *Photographer:* Louis G. Redstone.

WESTLAND CENTER, WESTLAND, MICHIGAN. *Architects:* Victor Gruen Associates; Louis G. Redstone Associates, Inc. *Artist:* Samuel Cashwan, "The Goose that Laid the Golden Egg," cast terrazzo, 10' x 5'; 1965. *Photographer:* Balthazar Korab.

EASTLAND CENTER, DETROIT, MICHIGAN. *Architects:* Victor Gruen Associates. *Artist:* Lindsey Decker, five-panel aluminum screen, 25' x 10'; 1957. *Photographer:* Louis G. Redstone.

WONDERLAND CENTER, LIVONIA, MICHIGAN. *Architects*: Louis G. Redstone Associates, Inc. *Artist*: Richard Jennings, glazed-brick mural, 80' x 12'; 1959. *Photographer*: David Kitz.

SOUTHLAND CENTER, HAYWARD, CALIFORNIA. *Architects*: John Graham & Company. *Artist*: François Stahly, wood sculpture, 30' high; 1962. *Photographer*: Louis G. Redstone.

WONDERLAND CENTER, LIVONIA, MICHIGAN. *Architects*: Louis G. Redstone Associates, Inc. *Artist*: Rosemary Zwick, "The Laughing Horse," concrete and ceramic sculpture, 7' high; 1959. *Photographer*: Louis G. Redstone.

WONDERLAND CENTER, LIVONIA, MICHIGAN. *Architects*: Louis G. Redstone Associates, Inc. *Artist*: Marjorie Kreilick, precast mural wall, 120' x 11'; 1959. *Photographer*: Louis G. Redstone.

GENERAL VIEW, WONDERLAND CENTER, LIVONIA, MICHIGAN. *Architects*: Louis G. Redstone Associates, Inc. *Artist*: Donald Buby, "The Rooster," metal sculpture, 6' high; 1959. *Photographer*: Balthazar Korab.

MAIN COURT, MACOMB MALL, ROSEVILLE, MICHIGAN. *Architects*: Louis G. Redstone Associates, Inc. *Artist*: Arthur Schneider, bronze fountain, 6'; 1965. *Photographer*: Daniel Bartush.

In the enclosed Westland Center the integration of the arts is used to great advantage to complement the architectural forms and to enhance the total environment. Serious works for interested adults are mixed with whimsical compositions and play sculptures for children to touch and enjoy. The character, size, and placement of the individual art pieces were carefully studied in relation to the whole interior. The plan of the center is based on two large courts and a connecting central mall. The visual reaction and images change as one walks from one court to the other. The entire setting of the art work is tied in with the floor design, landscaped spaces, and lighting effects.

In the open-mall Wonderland Center advantage is taken of the large unbroken exterior surfaces. Several glazed-brick murals were designed as an integral part of the structure, and a large precast concrete mural extends for 120 feet along one wall. The intricate patterns of the design for the brick murals were a challenge to the skill of the bricklayers, who took great pride in producing a colorful work of art. Here, also, the art program was integrated with the (outdoor) landscaped areas, the paving design, and the special lighting.

WESTLAND CENTER, WESTLAND, MICHIGAN. *Architects*: Victor Gruen Associates; Louis G. Redstone Associates, Inc. *Artist*: Samuel Cashwan, "Jack and the Beanstalk," metal sculpture, 20' high; 1965. *Photographer*: Balthazar Korab.

LIVONIA MALL, LIVONIA, MICHIGAN. *Architects*: Louis G. Redstone Associates, Inc. *Artist*: Morris Brose, bronze fountain, 7' x 5'; 1965. *Photographer*: Daniel Bartush.

NORTHLAND CENTER, SOUTHFIELD, MICHIGAN. *Architects*: Victor Gruen Associates. *Artist*: Marshall M. Fredericks, "Golden Boy," stone and bronze sculpture, 10' x 7'; 1954. *Photograph*: Courtesy of Marshall M. Fredericks.

Opposite:
ALA MOANA SHOPPING CENTER, HONOLULU, HAWAII. *Architects*: John Graham & Company. *Artist*: Bumpei Akaji, "Fountain of the Gods," mosaic and bronze column concealing a vent stack; each side of column designed to represent one of the four deities; gulls resting in water representing island theme; 1966. *Photographer*: David Cornwell.

ALA MOANA SHOPPING CENTER, HONOLULU, HAWAII. *Architects*: John Graham & Company. *Artist*: Alan Gerard, "Oahu Mural," bas-relief fresco map of Oahu; 1966. *Photographer*: David Cornwell.

ALA MOANA SHOPPING CENTER, HONOLULU, HAWAII. *Architects*: John Graham & Company. *Artist*: Claude Horan, "Fountain of the Twin Keikies," ceramic fountain inspired by the carefree spirit of play; 1966. *Photographer*: David Cornwell.

ALA MOANA SHOPPING CENTER, HONOLULU, HAWAII. *Architects*: John Graham & Company. *Artist*: Claude Horan, "Bamboo Fountain," ceramic figures and decorative tile symbolizing various cultures of the Pacific basin; 1966. *Photographers*: Camera Hawaii.

ALA MOANA SHOPPING CENTER, HONOLULU, HAWAII.
Architects: John Graham & Company. *Artist*: Claude Horan,
"Bamboo Fountain," ceramic figures and decorative tile symbolizing various cultures of the Pacific basin; 1966. *Photographer*: David Cornwell.

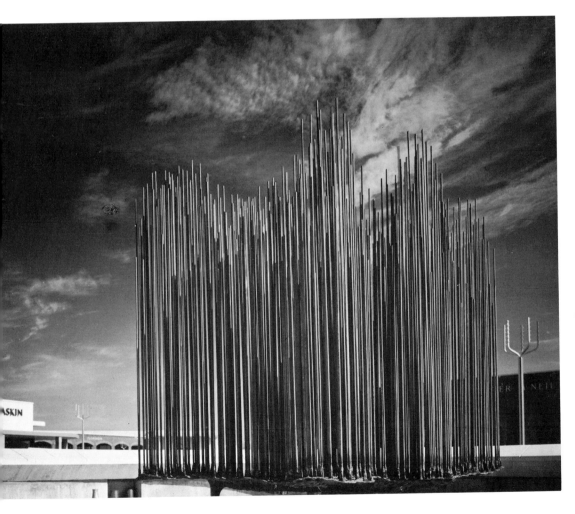

RIVER OAKS SHOPPING CENTER, CALUMET
CITY, ILLINOIS. *Architects*: Loebl Schlossman
Bennett & Dart. *Artist*: Harry Bertoia, sculptured
fountain, 9' 6" high x 8' 10" wide; 1966. *Photog-
phers*: Hube Henry, Hedrich-Blessing.

LLOYD CENTER, PORTLAND, OREGON. *Architects*: John Graham & Company. *Artist*: Ray Jensen, one of six "inferred" pools, 9' x 5' 3", created in vent holes; walls painted a very dark green-black color, which forms a striking background for sculptures; water inferred by fact that lily pads are all located in the same plane; bronze fish forms spring-mounted so that motion is created by air rising from level below; 1960. *Photograph*: Courtesy of John Graham & Company.

LLOYD CENTER, PORTLAND, OREGON. *Architects*: John Graham & Company. *Artist*: Tom Hardy, 1-ton steel sculpture composed of more than 300 bird forms 30' long, suspended from vaulted roof 40' above ice-skating pavilion; 1960. *Photograph*: Courtesy of John Graham & Company.

WEST MALL, LLOYD CENTER, PORTLAND, OREGON. *Architects*: John Graham & Company. *Artist*: George Tsutakawa, bronze fountain, 10' x 30'; 1960. *Photograph*: Courtesy of John Graham & Company.

FEDERAL BUILDINGS

The interest of our government in the integration of the arts in Federal buildings started in December, 1933, in the depth of the Depression, with the extensive and highly successful Works Progress Administration (WPA) program. The government's purpose of giving encouragement and employment to the American artist and, at the same time, of securing the best available American art for public buildings was well accomplished.

Among the several thousand commissions executed by the artists were murals and frescoes for many post office buildings, the Department of Justice building in Washington, D.C., and Federal housing and hospital projects, as well as many other forms of art work for auditoriums, lobbies, etc.[1]

One of the important benefits of this program was that the artist began to feel himself a part of the community which was backing him. This psychological factor of being needed is recognized to be as important as the actual security of being employed by the government.

Many of the 3,600 artists who participated in this program became nationally known, and to this day they have continued to contribute greatly to the development of the American art movement.

From the end of the WPA in 1942 until the 1960s, there was very little concern with the standards of art in Federal buildings, which for most communities meant a post office building. These buildings, moreover, were generally acquired by the government on a lease-construction or rental basis with minimum requirements for general design or art standards.

The year 1962 marked the beginning of a new approach by the Federal government to the architecture of its buildings. President

Kennedy's directive of May 23, "Guiding Principles for Federal Architecture," stressed a three-point policy:

1. The selection of distinguished designs that embody the finest contemporary American architectural thought.
2. The riddance of an official style and the encouragement of professional creativity through competitions and other means.
3. The special importance of landscaping and site development in relation to the surrounding area.

This order urged that funds totaling up to 1 percent of the construction cost of a new building project be reserved for the fine arts, the exact percentage to be determined by each agency head. The General Services Administration (GSA), which directs the largest building program in the Federal government, established an agency directive for the inclusion of reservations for fine arts amounting to ½ percent of the construction cost of structures of over $200,000, where appropriate.

According to Karel Yasko, Special Assistant to the Commissioner, Public Building Services, the effectiveness of the GSA in art and architecture since the Kennedy order can be seen in the number of works commissioned and in the quality of the artists chosen. Significant is the geographic distribution of the commissions, due largely to the fact that architects are finding talented artists in the general locale of their construction.

The procedure of award establishes certain checks without, however, placing any controls or restraints on the selected artist. The architect is requested by the GSA to submit a list of three artists and photographs of their work for approval by the Commission of Fine Arts. This approval concerns the quality of the artist; the final choice is a joint effort of the GSA and the architect, the contract being awarded by the GSA.

---

[1] Edward Bruce and Forbes Watsin, *Art in Federal Buildings*, Washington, D.C., 1936.

FEDERAL BUILDING, ST. LOUIS, MISSOURI. *Architects*: Murphy & Mackey. *Artist*: Robert Cronbach, "The Rivers," hammered and welded sheet-bronze fountain, 15' x 14'; 1963. *Photographer*: Robert Cronbach.

FEDERAL BUILDING, FORT WORTH, TEXAS. *Architect*: Thomas Stanley. *Artist*: Seymour Fogel, "The Challenge of Space," mural in ethyl šilicate, 14' x 32'; 1966. *Photographer*: Lee Angle.

DULLES INTERNATIONAL AIRPORT, WASHINGTON, D.C. *Architects*: Eero Saarinen & Associates. *Artist*: Harry Bertoia, cast bronze, 38' x 8'; 1962. *Photographer*: Balthazar Korab.

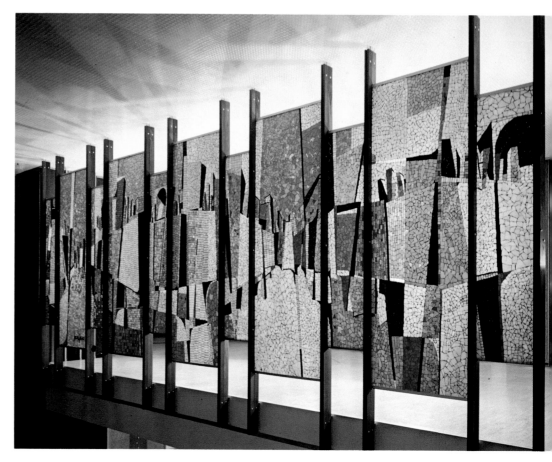

FEDERAL BUILDING, TAMPA, FLORIDA. *Architects*: Robert Wielage; H. Leslie Walker. *Artist*: Frank R. Prince, "The Endless City," glass mosaic murals consisting of six panels, 5' x 1' 2", and five panels, 6' 5" x 2' 5"; 1966. *Photographer*: G. Wade Swicord.

FEDERAL BUILDING, LOS ANGELES, CALIFORNIA. *Architects*: Welton Becket & Associates. *Coordinating Architects*: Albert C. Martin & Associates; Paul R. Williams & Associates. *Artist*: Richard Haines, glass mosaic murals; exterior panels, each 23' high x 29' long; interior mural, 9' 6" high x 47' long; theme, "Of the People, by the People and for the People"; 1964. *Photograph*: Courtesy of Richard Haines.

FEDERAL BUILDING, SALT LAKE CITY, UTAH. *Architects*: Snedaker & Budd. *Artist*: Angelo Caravaglia, precast stone sculpture group varying in height from 2' 6" to 12' 9"; 1966. *Photographer*: Richard K. Pollei.

FEDERAL COURTHOUSE AND OFFICE BUILDING, BILLINGS, MONTANA. *Architects*: J. G. Link & Company. *Artist*: Lyndon Fayne Pomeroy, "Philogenic Continuum," sculptured steel mural tracing development of region; five panels, each 8' 8" x 9' 6", weighing 3 tons; 1966. *Photograph*: Courtesy of Lyndon Fayne Pomeroy.

UNITED STATES COURTHOUSE AND FEDERAL BUILDING, DENVER, COLORADO. *Architects*: Fisher and Davis; James Sudler Associates. *Artist*: Robert I. Russin, carved wood reliefs; 1966. *Photographer*: Adele I. Russin.

LOBBY, JOHN F. KENNEDY FEDERAL CENTER, BOSTON MASSACHUSETTS. *Architects:* The Architects Collaborative, Inc. and Samuel Glaser. *Artist:* Robert Motherwell, mural; 1966. *Photographer:* Peter Main.

Above left and Left:
LOBBY, FEDERAL COURTHOUSE AND OFFICE BUILDING, RENO, NEVADA. *Architects:* Lockard, Parsons and Cazazza. *Artist:* Richard Guy Walton, oil-canvas mural, 6½' x 24½'; theme, "Birds, Wild Horses and Indian Spirit"; 1966. *Photographer:* Richard Guy Walton.

75

FEDERAL OFFICE BUILDING, KANSAS CITY, MISSOURI. *Architects*: Voskamp & Slezak; Everitt & Keleti; Radotinsky, Meyn, Deardorff, Howard, Needles, Tammen & Bergendoff. *Artist*: Costantino Nivola, concrete mural, 1,200 square feet; 1966. *Photograph*: Courtesy of Costantino Nivola.

RESIDENTIAL BUILDINGS

Adding the human touch of the artist to the intimate surroundings of the home reaches the very essence of good environment. It is also of paramount importance in creating a "climate" for the young of the family in which art is part of everyday living. It can be anticipated that many persons benefiting from this upbringing will in turn be torchbearers in seeking out and requiring beauty in their surroundings, whether in schools, business places, city plazas, or any other place in which they find themselves.

This book presents only a minute sampling of homes where architect and artist worked together successfully. Although these are homes in the higher-price bracket, the homeowner with a moderate budget can often establish contact with talented local artists whose works could bring great satisfaction to him.

The type of art used in the home takes many forms: murals on the larger wall areas; freestanding sculpture in the garden area, where it is related to landscaping and building; paved patio areas; and the design of draperies, rugs, and lighting fixtures. A renewed interest in the use of stained glass in homes is advocated by artist Joseph Escuder of Tampa, Florida: "The potentials of light managed thru stained glass haven't been explored as yet for homes—a shaft of light can be converted into a thing of beauty and inspiration for the person in the home—and the cost is comparatively minimal. . . ." Here again, as with other types of buildings, there are homes so designed that their shapes constitute sculptural forms in themselves. The enjoyment of the owner is as satisfactory an experience as reacting to a work of art.

Above and Below:
R. C. HOULAHAN RESIDENCE, BELLEVUE, WASHINGTON. *Architect*: John Anderson & Associates. *Artist*: Richard S. Beyer, custom-carved brick, part of fireplace lintel; 1966. *Photographer*: Art Holt.

DR. PAUL HENLEY RESIDENCE, EL DORADO, ARKANSAS. *Architect*: Fay Jones. *Artist*: Fay Jones, fountain sculpture, steel cage painted bronze color, 14' high; 1963. *Photographer*: Balthazar Korab.

It is interesting how often the lack of money results in something better than if funds had been available. On a recent dormitory project the budget that the Board of Trustees had authorized for sculpture and murals did not materialize. One day when the brick company salesman was in the office I asked him if he could get us a few green bricks to experiment on. He brought them, I laid them out on the drafting table at our coffee break, and several of us took knives, nails, beer can openers, thumbs and fingernails and produced the most spontaneous, unthought-out designs and sayings possible! We had these fired, the result being so pleasing, that I took several of my men down to the brick plant where we mutilated a couple of hundred bricks one afternoon. These were all finally burned and sent to the job where I culled about fifty percent of them before having the masons put them in the building walls. They are inserted in various places in the wall which you discover "accidentally" as you walk by. We hope that they will be a source of surprise and delight over the years to students who think "Art" is just for serious occasions. Poems were written, proverbs reproduced, both topical and enduring designs were made. I like to think that this almost casual communication across the generations has some value. . . .

Fred Bassetti

LT. COL. MARGARET D. HORN RESIDENCE, TUCSON, ARIZONA. *Architect*: Ann Rysdale. *Artist*: Erni Cabat, garden sculpture, cement cast in sand, 3' high; 1962. *Photograph*: Courtesy of Erni Cabat.

JACOB CAPIN RESIDENCE, NOGALES, ARIZONA. *Architect*: William Wilde. *Artist*: Erni Cabat, residential fixture for lighting; 1962. *Photographer*: Alfred A. Cohen.

. . . to earmark an entrance to a home "in the desert" where the home is several hundred feet away—there is no electricity to this spot and no water (maintenance must be at a minimum)—"Boomerang and Donut" designed as "point of awareness."

Daytime: Holes in "boomerang" contain stained glass—thru which at certain times of year (only), the sun will cast colored patterns on the wall.

Nighttime: Edges have pieces of colored glass and mirrors embedded in it—the reflections from the headlights of the car will highlight the piece and the wall.

The piece is cast in sand—shape is cantilevered out from the wall—welded armature extends thru cantilevered pipe and is attached thru back side of wall. . . .

Erni Cabat

BENJAMIN CAPIN RESIDENCE, NOGALES, ARIZONA. *Architect*: William Wilde. *Artist*: Erni Cabat, "Boomerang and Donut"; 1964. *Photograph*: Courtesy of Erni Cabat.

ARTHUR NEWFIELD RESIDENCE, LOS ANGELES, CALIFORNIA. *Architect*: Thornton Abell. *Artist*: Jane Ullman, sculpture for garden; 1961. *Photographer*: Julius Shulman.

HERBERT BROWNELL RESIDENCE, NEWPORT BEACH, CALIFORNIA. *Architect*: Herbert Brownell. *Artists*: Dextra Frankel and Charles Frankel, enamel-on-copper fountain; 1961. *Photographer*: Richard Gross.

W. HAWKINS FERRY RESIDENCE, GROSSE POINTE SHORES, MICHIGAN. *Architect*: Meathe, Kessler & Associates, Inc. *Artists*: Glen Michaels, mosaic terrace; Adolph Gottlieb, oil painting; 1964. *Photographer*: Balthazar Korab.

C. ALLEN HARLAN RESIDENCE, BLOOMFIELD HILLS, MICHIGAN. *Architect*: George Bery. *Artist*: Manola Pascual, "Goddess Pele and Crater Bird," wrought-iron sculpture, 8' high; 1962. *Photographer*: Tony Spina.

POLLOCK HOUSE, OKLAHOMA CITY, OKLAHOMA. *Architect*: Bruce Goff. *Photographer*: Joseph P. Messana.

VERA NEUMANN RESIDENCE, CROTON, NEW YORK. *Architect:* Marcel Breuer and Associates. *Artist:* Jan Peter Stern, spring stainless-steel laminations; 1961. *Photograph:* Courtesy of Jan Peter Stern.

MASLON RESIDENCE, PALM SPRINGS, CALIFORNIA. *Architect:* Richard Neutra, Inc. *Artist:* Kenneth Armitage, "Guardians," bronze garden sculpture, 3½′ x 4′; 1961. *Photographer:* Julius Shulman.

OUTER DRIVE EAST APARTMENT BUILDING, CHICAGO, ILLINOIS. *Architects*: Hirshfeld & Reinheimer; Pawlan Associates. *Artist*: Martin Reinheimer, cast-in-place sculptured balcony boxes, 17' long x 8' high x 5' deep; 1962. *Photographer*: Warren Meyer.

OUTER DRIVE EAST APARTMENT BUILDING, CHICAGO, ILLINOIS. *Architects*: Hirshfeld & Reinheimer; Pawlan Associates. *Artist*: Abbott Pattison, cast bronze sculpture, 19' x 12'; 1964. *Photographers*: Hedrich-Blessing.

PING YUEN ANNEX, SAN FRANCISCO, CALIFORNIA. *Owner*: Housing Authority of the City and County of San Francisco, California. *Architects*: John S. Bolles Associates. *Artist*: Ernest Born, sculptural frieze, 6' x 66'; 1963. *Photographer*: Pirkle Jones.

CAPITOL TOWERS, SACRAMENTO, CALIFORNIA. *Architects*: Wurster, Bernardi & Emmons; Edward L. Barnes; DeMars & Reay. *Artist*: Jacques Overhoff, sculptured precast concrete wall, 8' x 80'; 1961. *Photographer*: Morley Baer.

SOCIETY HILL APARTMENTS, PHILADELPHIA, PENNSYLVANIA. *Architects*: I. M. Pei & Associates. *Artist*: Leonard Baskin, bronze figures, larger than life size, of a seated man, a standing boy, and a bird figure, representing hopes and threats of the future; 1966. *Photograph*: Courtesy of Aluminum Company of America.

WILLIAM M. McVEY STUDIO-HOUSE, PEPPER PIKE, OHIO. *Architect*: R. A. Little. *Artist*: William M. McVey, "Birds in Flight," bronze cast over stainless-steel rod, 8' 6" high on granite base; 1953. *Photograph*: Courtesy of William M. McVey.

NATHAN CUMMINGS RESIDENCE, CHARLEVOIX, MICHIGAN. *Architect*: James F. Marshall. *Artist*: Walter Midener, Muntz-metal figure, 7' high; 1961. *Photograph*: Courtesy of Walter Midener.

PLAZAS AND MALLS

Today we proclaim our words to you people. In the squares and on the streets we are placing our work convinced that art must not remain a sanctuary. . . . Art should attend us everywhere that life flows and acts . . . at the bench, at the table, at work, at rest, at play; on working days and holidays . . . at home and on the road . . . in order that the flame to live should not extinguish in the mankind.

Naum Gabo

We are witnessing now in the United States a steady and definite migration from the rural to the urban areas. By 1980 the great majority of the United States population will be living in cities. If we are to make our cities more livable and provide for future facilities for physical and cultural developments, we cannot afford to procrastinate.

The replanning of our old cities and the planning of our new ones must be done with a long-range realistic view of combining sound economics and aesthetics. At the same time, this long-range plan has to have built-in factors of flexible change, expansion, and adaptability. The slow pace of this essential planning and the substitution of temporary face lifting or bulldozing of obsolete blocks have left most cities with ugly scars and still-unsolved problems. However, there is a beginning of recognition on the part of officials and responsible business leaders of the importance of embarking on a course of continued planning that would revitalize the cities and, at the same time, blend the old with the new.

According to Charles Blessing, director of the Detroit Planning Commission:

That all of these great cities have serious finance problems, no one can question. But the lesson is clear that just as hardheaded business corporations have of late acknowledged the value to them of beauty and of the public's good opinion of them, so too cities across the nation are now recognizing that the cultural climate of a city, the appearance of a city, the education and cultural facilities of a city—for music, drama, dance and all of the fine arts— are desirable not only because the people want them, need them, deserve them and insist on having them, but because it is good business for the city to provide them. Just as insurance companies and great industrial corporations must sell their image to their customers, the great American public, so too must cities now sell their image to these same great corporations and small ones too —as cities worth living in, working in, playing in, and investing in.

Art in the plazas and malls can become a stimulating and exhilarating experience in our urban environment. It can also create the individual character of a particular community.

The examples on the following pages show the excellent and extensive use made of sculpture, fountains, paving, play areas, landscaping, and lighting. There is no question that the enhanced surroundings create a feeling of enjoyment and pride in belonging to the community.

CONSTITUTION PLAZA, HARTFORD, CONNECTICUT.
Architect: Coordinating architect, Charles Dubose.
Landscape Architects: Sasaki, Dawson, DeMay & Associates, Inc. *Artist*: Masao Kinoshita, clock tower, steel frame faced with granite, 70' by 8'; 1964. *Photographers*: Hutchins Photography.

CONSTITUTION PLAZA, HARTFORD, CONNECTICUT. *Architect*: Coordinating architect, Charles Dubose. *Landscape Architects*: Sasaki, Dawson, DeMay & Associates, Inc. *Artist*: Masao Kinoshita, fountain; 1964. *Photographers*: Hutchins Photography.

GOLDEN GATEWAY CENTER, SAN FRANCISCO, CALIFORNIA. *Architects*: Wurster, Bernardi & Emmons. *Artist*: Seymour Lipton, "Pacific Bird," sculpture in metal, 2½' x 7'; 1965. *Photographers*: Dickey & Harleen Studios.

The art program in connection with the buildings and landscaped spaces was budgeted at 1 percent of construction costs (nearly $1 million), for sculptures, murals, fountains, and paintings. The art advisory committee included the director of the San Francisco Museum of Art, the director of the San Francisco Institute of Art, the director of the Palace of the Legion of Honor, and the chairman, who was a member of the development group.

The committee conducted an international competition for the design of a major sculpture for the Sydney Walton Square, a landscaped park, and selected François Stahly to install his "Fountain of the Four Seasons," which provides a water garden composed of stones and four geysers of sculptured bronze representing the seasons. The waters of the fountain cascade down to a labyrinth of stones in a tidal pool at the base. There are sitting space and climbing areas for children on the large granite blocks. The park is lighted by translucent globes hung on aluminum posts along the pathways.

Henry Moore's "Winged Figure" and a geometric bronze sculpture by Charles O. Perry, as well as a fountain designed by Woodward, Taranto and Wallace, were commissioned for the Maritime Plaza adjacent to the Alcoa office building. In addition to the art shown, a mosaic mural by Mark Adams in one apartment lobby and sculptures by D. Faralla and Alvin Light in two other residential lobbies, as well as paintings by Keith Boyle, Ralph Ducasse, and David Simpson, are part of the extensive art program of the Golden Gateway Center.

The Golden Gateway Center's remarkable use of art in a purely residential and office area could inspire similar ways of planning an environment where art is an essential part of daily living. A joint effort involving the best civic thinking of the developer and of representatives of the city planning commission, art authorities, and other interested organizations is a prerequisite for planning a wholesome and enjoyable environment.

GOLDEN GATEWAY CENTER, SAN FRANCISCO, CALIFORNIA. *Architects*: Wurster, Bernardi & Emmons. *Artist*: François Stahly, "Fountain of the Four Seasons," in the Sydney Walton Square, bronzed and carved stone with four spires, 13' to 17' high; 1965. *Photographers*: Dickey & Harleen Studios.

GOLDEN GATEWAY CENTER, SAN FRANCISCO, CALIFORNIA. *Architects*: Wurster, Bernardi & Emmons. *Artist*: Jacques Overhoff, bronze sculpture, 12' high, weighing over 5,000 pounds; 1965. *Photographers*: Dickey & Harleen Studios.

SOCIETY HILL APARTMENTS, PHILADELPHIA, PENNSYLVANIA. *Architect*: I. M. Pei & Associates. *Artist*: Gaston Lachaise, "The Floating Figure," bronze sculpture, 4' 4" x 8'; installed 1963. *Photograph*: Courtesy of Aluminum Company of America.

CLEVELAND WAR MEMORIAL FOUNTAIN, CIVIC CENTER MALL, CLEVELAND, OHIO. *Architects*: Roger Bailey; James Bennet Hughes. *Landscape Architects*: Clark and Rapuana. *Artist*: Marshall M. Fredericks, "The Fountain of Eternal Life," bronze central figure, 35' high; bronze filigreed sphere, 10½' in diameter; 1964. *Photographer*: Maurice C. Hartwick.

ASPEN MEADOWS HOTEL DEVELOPMENT, ASPEN, COLORADO. *Architect*: Herbert Bayer. *Artist*: Herbert Bayer, marble garden, 36' x 36'; 1955. *Photographers*: Berko Photo.

THE MALL, FRESNO, CALIFORNIA. *Architects*: Victor Gruen Associates. *Landscape Architects*: Eckbo, Dean, Austin & Williams. *Artist*: Jan De Swart, freestanding clock sculpture, 59' x 4' 6"; 1964. *Photographers*: Tidyman Studios.

Some of the most critical problems in the development of Fresno Mall were the street closures, the necessity of obtaining enabling legislation (an effort actually led by the city of Pomona), the task of establishing an assessment district to include all property owners to be benefited by the Mall, the necessity of enlarging the boundaries of the central-business-district redevelopment project, the methods of financing and phasing new parking facilities, and the resolution of final freeway alignments. The Mall, though it constitutes only one part of the plans for revitalizing the central area and only a small part of the programmed public and private investments, expresses most clearly the basic philosophy which guided the shaping of the vision:

It is built with both public and private funds.

Its construction required both public and private approval.

Together with the adjoining alleys and streets, it defines a separation of pedestrian from automobile, as well as a separation of truck and bus traffic.

It is designed to accommodate new buildings alongside existing structures.

It demonstrates that beauty can be part of sound economic and functional city planning.

THE MALL, FRESNO, CALIFORNIA. *Architects*: Victor Gruen Associates. *Landscape Architects*: Eckbo, Dean, Austin & Williams. *Artist*: Stanley C. Bitters, "Dancing Waters," fired-clay (ceramic) fountain sculpture, 4' x 25' 3" x 40' 6"; 1964. *Photographer*: Franklin Boruszak.

Artist: Newton T. Russell, "Trisem," granite sculpture, 11' high; 1965.

Artist: George Tsutakawa, "Obos," bronze-plate fountain sculpture, 9' high; 1964.

THE MALL, FRESNO, CALIFORNIA. *Architects:* Victor Gruen Associates. *Landscape Architects:* Eckbo, Dean, Austin & Williams. *Photographer:* Franklin Boruszak (above and below left).

Artist: Clement Renzi, "The Visit," bronze sculpture, 7' x 6' x 4'; 1965.

Artist: Charles Owen Perry, "Ellipsoid VI," placed in Fulton Mall, brass plate, 4' high, 6' in diameter; 1964. *Photograph:* Courtesy of Fresno City-County Chamber of Commerce.

95

CONVENTION CENTER, THE MALL, FRESNO, CALIFORNIA. *Architects:* Adrian Wilson & Associates; Robert Stevens Associates. *Landscape Architects:* Eckbo, Dean, Austin & Williams. *Artist:* Alexander Calder, "Bucephalus," steel-plate sculpture, 9'3" x 16'5" x 14'2"; 1963. *Photographer:* Franklin Boruszak.

THE MALL, FRESNO, CALIFORNIA. *Architects:* Victor Gruen Associates. *Landscape Architects:* Eckbo, Dean, Austin & Williams. *Artist:* Claire Falkenstein, "Leaping Fire," placed in Fulton Mall, 18' x 5' 2" x 6' 9"; 1966. *Photograph:* Courtesy of Fresno City-County Chamber of Commerce.

THE MALL, FRESNO, CALIFORNIA. *Architects:* Victor Gruen Associates. *Landscape Architects:* Eckbo, Dean, Austin & Williams. *Artist:* Peter Voulkos, "Big A," placed in Mariposa Mall, 9' x 4' x 6'; 1965. *Photograph:* Courtesy of Fresno City-County Chamber of Commerce.

CHILDREN'S PLAY AREA, THE MALL, FRESNO, CALIFORNIA. *Architects:* Victor Gruen Associates. *Landscape Architects:* Eckbo, Dean, Austin & Williams. *Artists:* Creative Playthings, Inc., cast concrete play sculpture; 1966. *Photographer:* Gordon Sommers. *Photograph:* Courtesy of Fresno City-County Chamber of Commerce.

OFFICE BUILDINGS AND BANKS

Whatever the motivations of the American corporations and businessmen in their comparatively recent interest in the inclusion of art in their building programs, it is a heartening and encouraging development. Not only does this interest in art create a favorable image for them, but it contributes to the cultural life of the community through visible means. Economics should not be the only concern of business. As John Kenneth Galbraith, professor of economics at Harvard University, says, "We must explicitly assert the claims of beauty against those of economics. That something is cheaper, more convenient or more efficient is no longer decisively in its favor." The truth of this statement is borne out by the fact that business has gained in sales and popularity through the stimulation of beauty.

Although the examples of art shown here generally form an integral part of the structure or of the building complex, there are other manifestations of interest by the business world which ultimately may lead to the ideal merger of the arts and architecture. These are buying and exhibiting art collections, using works of art in executive and public spaces, and offering awards to exhibiting artists. However, in the final analysis it must be the architect who initiates the planning of an art program for his clients. The architect's personal interest, his enthusiasm, and his contact with talented local artists are a prerequisite for successful results.

In my own experience with the executives of banks and corporations, I have found a favorable response to the idea of incorporating art in buildings. In one case in which similar plans for branch-bank office buildings were used, the individual character of each branch was expressed by a different art approach. For example, a different artist was commissioned to design an ornamental screen in front of each safety deposit vault. Also, the murals on the walls in back of the tellers, which face the public, were designed by different artists.

Above all, it is important that the artist and the architect have a meeting of minds and a good working relationship for satisfactory results.

McGRAW-HILL BOOK COMPANY, CORTE MADERA, CALIFORNIA. *Architects*: John S. Bolles Associates. *Artist*: Harry Crotty, metal-sculpture screen, 10' x 25'; 1960. *Photographer*: Pirkle Jones.

11000 McNICHOLS BUILDING, DETROIT, MICHIGAN. *Architect*: Louis G. Redstone Associates, Inc. *Artist*: Malcolm Moran, stainless-steel sculpture, 10' high; 1962. *Photographer*: David Kitz.

PEACHTREE CENTER OFFICE BUILDING, ATLANTA, GEORGIA. *Architects*: Edwards & Portman. *Artist*: Robert Helsmoortel, freestanding sculpture, approximately 40' high; 1965. *Photographers*: Clyde May Photography, Inc.

SUN LIFE INSURANCE BUILDING, BALTIMORE, MARYLAND. *Architects*: Peterson & Brickbauer. *Artist*: Dimitri Hadzi, "Helios," sculpture; 1966. *Photographers*: Joseph W. Molitor Photography.

CROCKER CITIZENS BANK, SACRAMENTO, CALIFORNIA. *Architects*: John S. Bolles Associates. *Artist*: David Tolerton, colored-marble-chip–plaster background with anodized-aluminum forms, 12' x 180'; 1963. *Photographer*: Pirkle Jones.

Above and Below:
ARIZONA BANK, TUCSON, ARIZONA. *Architects*: Friedman & Jobusch. *Artist*: Ron Boice, "Family Group," sculpture; tallest figure, 8'; 1963. *Photographers*: Manley Commercial Photography.

INTERNATIONAL BUSINESS MACHINES CORPORATION, SAN JOSE, CALIFOR-NIA. *Architects*: John S. Bolles Associates. *Artist*: Keith Monroe, "Reeds," flexible tubes, 15' high, that vibrate in a breeze, producing sound and also ripples on the pool's surface; 1957. *Photographer*: Pirkle Jones.

INTERNATIONAL BUSINESS MACHINES CORPORATION, SAN JOSE, CALIFOR-NIA. *Architects*: John S. Bolles Associates. *Artist*: Robert B. Howard, "Hydro-Gyro," in which stars revolve and sway with the wind to constantly changing positions, planes, and interrelationships, 40' high; 1957. *Photographer*: Pirkle Jones.

INTERNATIONAL MONETARY FUND, WASHINGTON, D.C. *Architects:* Clas, Riggs, Owen & Ramos. *Consulting Architect:* Vincent Kling. *Artist:* Glen Michaels, mosaic mural in terrazzo marble, bronze, and tile, 10' x 37'; 1966. *Photographer:* Balthazar Korab.

ROHM AND HAAS BUILDING, PHILADELPHIA, PENNSYLVANIA. *Architects:* George M. Ewing Company. *Consulting Architect:* Pietro Belluschi. *Artist:* Freda Koblick, cast acrylic mural with color, 9' x 11'; 1965. *Photographer:* David Marston.

PAN AMERICAN WORLD AIRWAYS BUILDING, GRAND CENTRAL BUILDING, INC., NEW YORK CITY. *Architects:* Emery Roth & Sons. *Design Consultants:* Walter Gropius (The Architects Collaborative, Inc.); Pietro Belluschi. *Artist:* Josef Albers, laminated-plastic mural, 60' x 27'; 1963. *Photographer:* Louis G. Redstone.

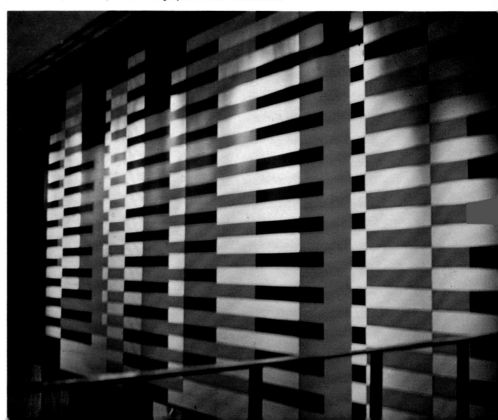

LYTTON SAVINGS & LOAN ASSOCIATION OF NORTHERN CALIFORNIA, OAKLAND, CALIFORNIA. *Architect*: Kurt Meyer & Associates. *Artist*: George Rickey, stainless steel with 150 moving rotors, 15' high x 32' wide overall, weighing 1½ tons; 1965. *Photographer*: Julius Shulman.

GENERAL MOTORS TECHNICAL CENTER, WARREN, MICHIGAN. *Architects*: Eero Saarinen & Associates. *Artist*: Antoine Pevsner, oxidized-bronze sculpture, 16' high; 1955. *Photographer*: Joseph P. Messana.

PRUDENTIAL FEDERAL SAVINGS & LOAN BUILDING, SALT LAKE CITY, UTAH. *Architects*: William L. Pereira & Associates. *Artist*: Tom Van Sant, "Birds in Flight," 100 birds with wingspread of 4', attached to three bronze-encased stainless-steel rods, each 120' high (electrodeposited-bronze process developed from the aircraft industry); theme symbolic of seagulls which saved Mormon crops by eating locusts; 1964. *Photographer*: Julius Shulman.

GATEWAY BUILDING, CENTURY CITY, LOS ANGELES, CALIFORNIA. *Architects*: Welton/Becket & Associates. *Artist*: Bernard Rosenthal, "Walls of Shadows," two black aluminum walls, 13' high x 35' wide; 1963. *Photographer*: Julius Shulman.

MAIN OFFICE, MEDUSA PORTLAND CEMENT ASSOCIATION BUILDING, CLEVELAND, OHIO. *Architects*: Rowley, Payer, Huffman & Leithold, Inc. *Artists*: William M. McVey, precast wall composed of 3' x 3' elements; 1957. *Photographers*: Hube Henry, Hedrich-Blessing.

HEADQUARTERS BUILDING, CALIFORNIA CONGRESS OF PARENTS AND TEACHERS, LOS ANGELES, CALIFORNIA. *Architects*: Smith, Powell & Morgridge. *Artist*: Tom Van Sant, relief carving in Mexican handmade-brick screen walls, each 9′ 6″ x 50′ 4″; 1961. *Photographer*: Larry Frost. *Photograph*: Courtesy of Powell, Morgridge, Richards & Coghlan.

As in any work of art, there are many meanings to this work. There is first of all the formal one of compositional relationship to the rest of the design (the garden), which in turn is governed by the architecture which sets the pace. . . . The matter of scale, the material, the manner of working, all are aspects of this single problem. It would be difficult to say what is the true and deepest meaning. I like to think of this as closer to psychology and not so easily expressible strivings—whose expression can only be adequately discerned in the viewing of the sculpture. . . .

May I say that the placing of stone on stone has its own mystical meaning. It is among the earliest marks left by man to denote his striving after security and order, his conquest over the chaos and uncertainty of existence. Architecture is itself an embodiment of this—as is also a well-ordered life. I suppose this is the basic desire upon which insurance companies are founded—which makes the Elements pertinent here.

Isamu Noguchi

CONNECTICUT GENERAL LIFE INSURANCE COMPANY, BLOOMFIELD, CONNECTICUT. *Architects:* Skidmore, Owings & Merrill. *Artist:* Isamu Noguchi, "The Family," red granite sculpture group of three monoliths, 16' x 8' 6", 8' 3" x 7', and 12' x 7'; 1957. *Photographers:* Ezra Stoller Associates.

DEERE & COMPANY ADMINISTRATIVE CENTER, MOLINE, ILLINOIS. *Architect*: Eero Saarinen & Associates. *Artist*: Alexander Girard, mural in two units, each 87' x 9' 6''; 1964. *Photographers*: Ezra Stoller Associates.

GENERAL AMERICAN LIFE INSURANCE COMPANY BUILDING, ST. LOUIS, MISSOURI. *Architects*: Wedemeyer and Hecker. *Artist*: Rodney M. Winfield, "Life Symbols," bronze and steel sculpture, 5' x 6'; 1952. *Photographer*: Chester Danett.

THOMAS J. WATSON RESEARCH CENTER, INTERNATIONAL BUSINESS MACHINES CORPORATION,
YORKTOWN HEIGHTS, NEW YORK. *Architect*: Eero Saarinen & Associates. *Artist*: Seymour Lipton,
freestanding bronze sculpture, 5′ high x 8′ long; 1960. *Photographer*: R. W. Collier.

CENTRAL NATIONAL LIFE INSURANCE GROUP BUILDING, OMAHA, NEBRASKA. *Architects*: Leo
A. Daly Company. *Artist*: Bill J. Hammon, sculptured concrete panels, 4' x 8'; 1961. *Photographers*:
Chapman/Spittler Productions, Inc.

INTERNATIONAL BUSINESS MACHINES HEADQUARTERS BUILDING, LOS ANGELES, CALIFORNIA. *Architects*: William L. Pereira & Associates; Charles Luckman Associates. *Artist*: Bernard Rosenthal, bronze sculpture, 9' high x 12' wide; 1954. *Photographer*: Marvin Rand.

CROCKER CITIZENS NATIONAL BANK, SACRAMENTO, CALIFORNIA. *Architects*: John S. Bolles Associates. *Artist*: Louis Beardslee III, cast aluminum chandelier, 8' long x 5' high, weighing approximately 1,000 pounds; 1965. *Photographer*: Pirkle Jones.

PATIO, OFFICE BUILDING, LOUIS G. REDSTONE ASSOCI-
ATES, INC., DETROIT, MICHIGAN. *Architects*: Louis G.
Redstone Associates, Inc. *Landscape Architects*: Milton Baron
and Hrand Hampikian. *Artists*: Julius Schmidt, bronzed-steel
gate, 5' x 7'; Samuel Cashwan, ceramic fountain figures;
1954. *Photographers*: Lens-Art Studio.

PAN AMERICAN WORLD AIRWAYS BUILDING, GRAND CENTRAL
BUILDING, INC., NEW YORK CITY. *Architects*: Emery Roth & Sons.
Consulting Architects: The Architects Collaborative, Inc. *Artist*: Richard
Lippold, wire sculpture in the lobby of Vanderbilt Avenue, 30' high x
60' long; 1963. *Photographer*: J. Alex Langley.

PLAZA, DENVER UNITED STATES NATIONAL BANK CEN-
TER, DENVER, COLORADO. *Architects*: I. M. Pei (original
Mile High Center); James Sudler Associates (renamed Denver
United States National Bank Center), with alterations and
additions. *Artist*: Edgar Britton, "Tower of Prometheus,"
bronze, 25' high; 1965. *Photographer*: Ellen Wagstaff.

UNITED STATES PLYWOOD BUILDING, NEW YORK CITY. *Architect*: William Lescaze. *Artist*: Beverly Pepper, "Contrapunto," stainless-steel sculpture, 18' x 18' x 18'; 1963. *Photographers*: Ezra Stoller Associates.

MANUFACTURERS HANOVER TRUST COMPANY, TIME-LIFE BUILDING, NEW YORK CITY. *Architects*: Harrison, Abramovitz & Harris. *Artist*: Gyorgy Kepes, mural screen of faceted colored glass, including 15,000 pieces and 9,000 gold-inlay pieces; 1959. *Photographers*: Ezra Stoller Associates.

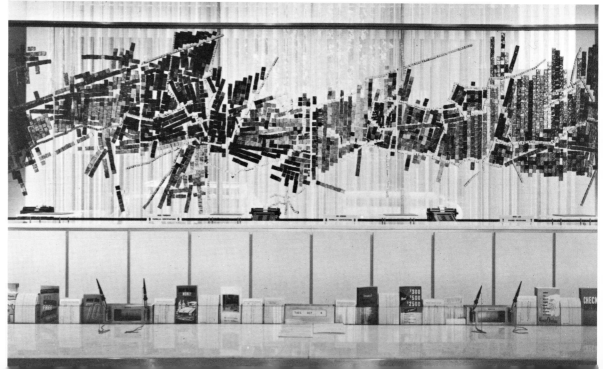

AMERICAN REPUBLIC INSURANCE COMPANY, DES MOINES, IOWA. *Architects*: Skidmore, Owings & Merrill. *Artist*: Alexander Calder, "Spunk of the Monk," steel sculpture, 11½' high x 24' long; 1964. *Photographer*: Larry Day.

HOFFMANN—LA ROCHE PHARMACEUTICAL COMPANY, NUTLEY, NEW JERSEY. *Architects*: Wigton-Abbott Corporation. *Artist*: James Wines, bronze sculpture, diameters of 10', 8' and 5'; 1965. *Photographer*: O. E. Nelson. *Photograph*: Courtesy of Marlborough-Gerson Gallery, Inc., New York.

I usually avoid forcing my materials beyond the elastic limits—which in the case of spring steel are very high. This may be an avoidance of violence. Yet, to form a sculpture I may use all my forces, or those of machines of my devising, to set against one another the forces pent up within the sculpture. It may be akin to tuning of a stringed instrument. Music was my first goddess. Through my sculptures and poems I come as close as I may ever be able to, to composing music. Sculpture, more so than the graphic art forms, may be a closer mate to musical composition in that it must also be experienced sequentially; one walks about it, feels the vibrations of the wind, observes the changes produced by shifting sun and clouds.

I like the hardness of stainless steel; to wrest huge sheets into shape. The form takes on its character all at once! The luminous liquid quality of stainless gives it a life of its own. The lyric Wind Shapes I envision to be poised in balance—stirred by the winds that course over the land, yet resistant to storms and man. Their sinuous and elusive surfaces shift in emphasis through the movement of the observer and obtain coloring by variation in natural lighting.

Jan Peter Stern

PRUDENTIAL CENTER, BOSTON, MASSACHUSETTS. *Architects*: Charles Luckman Associates. *Artist*: Jan Peter Stern, "Limits of Horizon," stainless-steel sculpture, 7' high x 19' long; 1966. *Photographer*: Gordon N. Converse, *The Christian Science Monitor*.

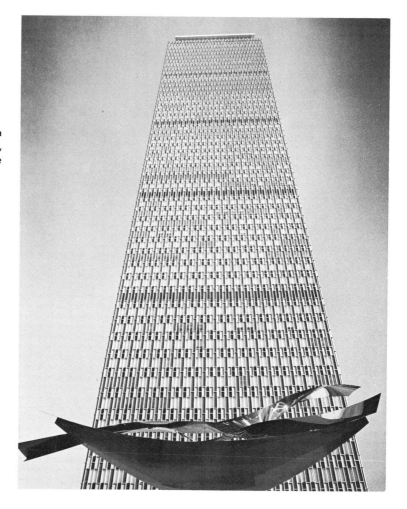

PHOENIX MUTUAL LIFE INSURANCE COMPANY BUILDING, HARTFORD, CONNECTICUT. *Architects*: Harrison & Abramovitz. *Artist*: Roy Gussow, "Mutual," stainless-steel sculpture, 8' x 5'; 1964. *Photographers*: Joseph W. Molitor Photography. Below: *Photographers*: Edward Saxe Studio.

MUTUAL INSURANCE COMPANY OF HARTFORD BUILDING, HARTFORD, CONNECTICUT. *Architects*: Sherwood, Mills & Smith. *Artist*: Costantino Nivola, bas-relief mural, 110' x 30'; 1958. *Photographer*: Robert L. Nay.

INTERNATIONAL BUSINESS MA-CHINES PLAZA, SEATTLE, WASH-INGTON. *Architect*: Minoru Yamasaki. *Associate Architects*: Naramore, Bain, Brady & Johanson. *Artist*: James Fitzgerald, sculptured bronze fountain, 7' x 8' x 22'; 1965. *Photographers*: Dudley, Hardin & Yang, Inc.

LOBBY, HOFFMANN–LA ROCHE PHARMACEUTICAL COMPANY, NUTLEY, NEW JERSEY. *Architects*: Wigton-Abbott Corporation. *Artist*: Seymour Fogel, "Research and the Universe," sand and epoxy mural, 22' high x 35' long; 1964. *Photographer*: Eric Pollitzer.

PURITAN CENTER BUILDING, DETROIT, MICHIGAN. *Architects*: Louis G. Redstone Associates, Inc. *Artist*: Louis G. Redstone, mosaic mural, 14' x 10'; 1959. *Photographers*: Lens-Art Studio.

HIRAM WALKER RECEPTION CENTER, WALKERVILLE, ONTARIO, CANADA. *Architects*: Smith, Hinchman & Grylls Associates, Inc. *Artists*: David Partridge, copper, steel, and aluminum nail configuration, 20' high (above); Jean D'Arc Carriveau, tapestry, designed and woven by artist, 10' x 20' (below); 1965. *Photographer*: Bob Wallace.

NORTHWESTERN LIFE INSURANCE BUILDING, MINNEAPOLIS, MINNESOTA. *Architect*: Minoru Yamasaki & Associates. *Artist*: Harry Bertoia, metal screen, brass-coated steel with bronze-tipped rods, 46′ x 13′ x 3½′; 1964. *Photographer*: Balthazar Korab.

FIRST NATIONAL CITY BANK, NEW YORK CITY. *Architect*: Raoul Du Brul, consultant. *Designers*: Raymond Loewy/William Snaith, Inc., sculptured carpet hung as a mural, 9′ x 24′; 1964. *Photographers*: Gottscho-Schleisner, Inc.

LOS ANGELES ATHLETIC CLUB, LOS ANGELES, CALIFORNIA. *Architect*: Faxon, Gruys & Saylor. *Interior Designer*: Rex Davis. *Artists*: Dextra Frankel and Charles Frankel, copper screen; 1965. *Photographer*: Julius Shulman.

LOBBY, GROWTH SCIENCES CENTER, INTERNATIONAL MINERALS & CHEMICAL CORPORATION, LIBERTYVILLE, ILLINOIS. *Architects*: Wigton-Abbott Corporation. *Consulting Architects*: Perkins & Will. *Artist*: Buell Mullen, stainless-steel mural, 10′ x 23′; weighing 1,000 pounds; theme, "Tree of Life and Chemical Molecular Forms Essential to Plant Growth"; 1966. *Photograph*: Courtesy of International Minerals & Chemical Corporation.

LOS ANGELES ATHLETIC CLUB, LOS ANGELES, CALIFORNIA. *Architect*: Faxon, Gruys & Saylor. *Interior Designer*: Rex Davis. *Artists*: Dextra Frankel and Charles Frankel, copper panel; 1965. *Photographer*: Julius Shulman.

PACIFIC EMPLOYERS GROUP INSURANCE COMPANY, LOS ANGELES, CALIFORNIA. *Architects*: Charles Luckman Associates. *Artist*: Ellamarie Wooley and Jackson Wooley, "Pacificana," enamel and copper mural, 10' x 24'; 1963. *Photographers*: Vanguard Photography.

LINDELL TERRACE RESTAURANT, LINDELL TERRACE APARTMENTS, ST. LOUIS, MISSOURI. *Architects*: Helmuth, Obata & Kassabaum. *Artist*: Freda Koblick, "Mississippi Riverboat," cast acrylic wall panel, 10' x 10'; 1963. *Photographers*: W. C. Runder Photo Company, Inc.

SAN FRANCISCO HILTON, SAN FRANCISCO, CALIFORNIA. *Architects*: Tabler & Tabler. *Artist*: Janet Bennett, twenty-four semihardwood screens, each 5' x 11'; 1965. *Photographer*: Ashworth of London.

ADMINISTRATION BUILDING, OLDSMOBILE DIVISION, GENERAL MOTORS CORP., LANSING, MICHIGAN. *Architects*: Argonaut Realty Division, General Motors Corp. *Artist*: Samuel Cashwan, copper-clad steel sculpture, 17' high; 1966. *Photographer*: Harry B. Starling.

CIBA PHARMACEUTICAL COMPANY, SUMMIT, NEW JERSEY. *Architects*: Eggers & Higgins. *Artist*: N. H. Azaz, precast concrete sculpture, 12' x 4' x 3'; 1965. *Photographer*: Bill Mechnick. *Photograph*: Courtesy of Estelle Dodge Associates, Incorporated.

INLAND STEEL BUILDING, CHICAGO, ILLINOIS. *Architects*: Skidmore, Owings & Merrill. *Artist*: Richard Lippold, "The Radiant Eye," sculpture of stainless-steel tubes and coated and uncoated stainless-steel wires, 13' high from floor of reflecting pool to dropped ceiling, out-to-out dimensions are 15' x 23'; 1958. *Photographers*: Hedrich-Blessing.

DETROIT BANK & TRUST, CLINTON TOWN-SHIP, MICHIGAN. *Architects*: Louis G. Redstone Associates, Inc. *Artist*: Narendra Patel, carved wood screen, 12' x 7'; 1966. *Photographer*: Robert Vigiletti.

DETROIT BANK & TRUST, WESTLAND, MICHIGAN. *Architects*: Louis G. Redstone Associates, Inc. *Artist*: Irving Berg, metal welded screen, 12' x 7'; *Photographer*: Daniel Bartush.

FIRST FEDERAL BANK, DETROIT, MICHIGAN. *Architects*: Louis G. Redstone Associates, Inc. *Artist*: Samuel Cashwan, metal mural, 25' x 4'; 1966. *Photographer*: Balthazar Korab.

BANK OF AMERICA, SAN MATEO, CALIFORNIA. *Architects*: Wurster, Bernardi & Emmons. *Artist*: Louis Macouillard, mosaic depicting life of founder, A. P. Giannini, 24' high; 1963. *Photographer*: Roger Sturtevant.

SECURITY LIFE & ACCIDENT COMPANY BUILDING, DENVER, COLORADO. *Architects*: Sorey, Hill & Sorey. *Artist*: Vincent O'Brien, sculptured murals, precast reinforced concrete, 6½' x 20'; 1964. *Photographer*: Vincent O'Brien.

FIRST NATIONAL BANK BUILDING, SAN DIEGO, CALIFORNIA. *Architects*: Tucker, Sadler & Bennett. *Artists*: Ellamarie Wooley and Jackson Wooley, "Variations on a Gold Theme," enamel and copper mural, 12' x 36'; 1965. *Photographers*: Buxco-Nestor Professional Photographic Services.

MANUFACTURERS NATIONAL BANK, WESTLAND CENTER, WESTLAND, MICHIGAN. *Architects*: Louis G. Redstone Associates, Inc. *Artist*: Narendra Patel, bronze-wire composition, 6' x 30'; 1966. *Photographer*: Robert Vigiletti.

11000 WEST McNICHOLS BUILDING, DETROIT, MICHIGAN. *Architects*: Louis G. Redstone Associates, Inc. *Artist*: Louis G. Redstone, brick design on 70' x 35' wall; 1961. *Photographer*: David Kitz.

HARLAN BUILDING, BIRMINGHAM, MICHIGAN. *Architects*: Louis G. Redstone Associates, Inc. *Artist*: Arthur Schneider, chromium-plated metal relief, 8' x 10'; 1961. *Photographer*: David Kitz.

THE OKLAHOMA PUBLISHING COMPANY BUILDING, OKLAHOMA CITY, OKLAHOMA. *Architects*: Sorey, Hill, Binicker. *Artist*: Bernard Frazer, figures representing "Investigation, Analysis, Exposition," copper on stainless steel, 16' high; 1964. *Photograph*: Courtesy of the Oklahoma Publishing Company.

I have estimated that 90% of the vision moments for any sculpture now are directed from automotive positions. My sculptures therefore—involve all directions—vision potential—and gesture moves as the eye passes by them.

Bernard Frazer

Each of the three sculptures was constructed from a model one-fourth the size of the completed figure. The inside structure of each figure was formed entirely of stainless steel, consisting of a central core with hundreds of spokes radiating outward. Copper sheets were then welded around the skeleton of steel. By means of a helioarc, the copper exterior was given a final appearance which looks much like molten metal. The head, hands, and feet, which were made of cast bronze, were also given this treatment.

UNITED NATIONS HEADQUARTERS

It seemed natural to conclude Part I with the art in the buildings of the United Nations. Art in all its forms has a universal appeal and the unique quality of bringing people of all races and creeds together in warm camaraderie, fostering tolerance and understanding. If ever there was a building, or group of buildings, which needed this marriage of art and architecture, it was the United Nations complex.

The very essence of the purpose of the United Nations—the pursuit of peace and happiness for all nations—prompted the many members to commission their best artists to design works for the various areas of the buildings.

Even though the theme of "peace" and the "progress of mankind" prevails in most of the art work, the variety of approaches as interpreted by the artists of different nationalities creates an immense interest.

The art works, some sixty in number, range from small paintings to vast murals; from delicate carvings to heavy doors; from the art of 3,000 years ago to contemporary contributions; from a figure of a priestess carved in satinwood, representing peace, to large murals, representing war and peace, by the Brazilian artist Candido Portinari; from a fountain donated by the schoolchildren of the United States, Puerto Rico, and the Virgin Islands to a sculptured figure of a man beating his sword into a plowshare by the Russian sculptor Evgeniy Vuchetich. Space does not allow us to give a complete listing of the art works. The following illustrations show a representative cross section. Not all are perfect examples of the integration of art and architecture, but they are shown here nevertheless because of the special significance of the United Nations concept. There is still need for outside art work in scale and scope befitting this important complex of buildings. Hopefully, this will be created in the near future.

GENERAL ASSEMBLY BUILDING, UNITED NATIONS HEADQUARTERS, NEW YORK CITY. *Architects*: International team of fourteen consultants; director of planning, Wallace K. Harrison; deputy director of planning, Max Abramovitz. *Artist*: Peter Golf, Belgian, woven tapestry, 43½' x 28½'; theme, "Peace, Prosperity and Equality"; 1954. *Photograph*: Courtesy of United Nations.

Below:
UNITED NATIONS HEADQUARTERS, NEW YORK CITY. *Architects*: International team of fourteen consultants; director of planning, Wallace K. Harrison; deputy director of planning, Max Abramovitz. *Artist*: Barbara Hepworth, English, "Single Form," bronze, 21'; 1964. *Photograph*: Courtesy of United Nations.

UNITED NATIONS HEADQUARTERS, NEW YORK CITY. *Architects*: International team of fourteen consultants; director of planning, Wallace K. Harrison; deputy director of planning, Max Abramovitz. *Artist*: Evgeniy Vuchetich, Russian, bronze sculpture, "Let Us Beat Swords into Ploughshares," 9' 6"; 1959. *Photograph*: Courtesy of United Nations.

Opposite:
GENERAL ASSEMBLY BUILDING, UNITED NATIONS HEADQUARTERS, NEW YORK CITY. *Architects*: International team of fourteen consultants; director of planning, Wallace K. Harrison; deputy director of planning, Max Abramovitz. *Artist*: Fernand Léger, French, mural in orange, white, and dark gray, executed by Bruce Gregory, 33' x 28'; 1962. *Photograph*: Courtesy of United Nations.

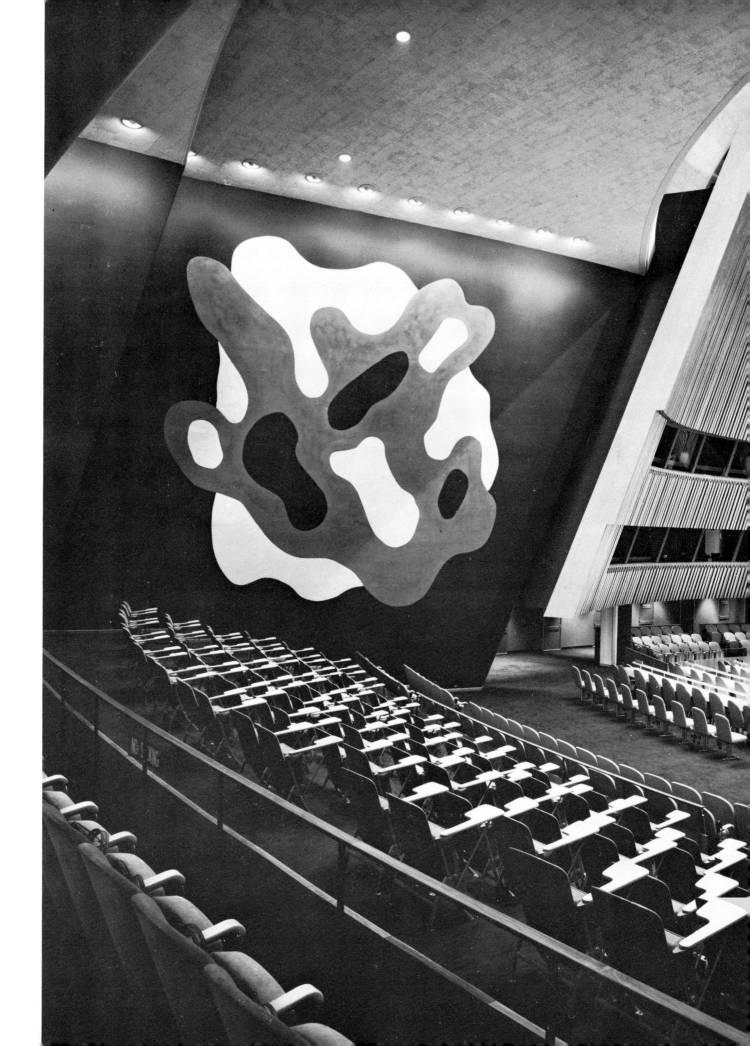

LOBBY, MEDITATION ROOM, UNITED NATIONS HEAD-QUARTERS, NEW YORK CITY. *Architects*: International team of fourteen consultants; director of planning, Wallace K. Harrison; deputy director of planning, Max Abramovitz. *Artist*: Robert Cronbach, American, sculpture of hammered and welded sheet, bronze, brass, and stainless steel, 8' long; 1960. *Photographer*: Eric Pollitzer.

CONFERENCE BUILDING, UNITED NATIONS HEADQUARTERS, NEW YORK CITY. *Architects*: International team of fourteen consultants; director of planning, Wallace K. Harrison; deputy director of planning, Max Abramovitz. *Artist*: José Vela Zanetti, Spanish, mural, 60' x 12'; theme, "Mankind's Struggle for Lasting Peace"; 1953. *Photograph*: Courtesy of United Nations.

DAG HAMMARSKJOLD LIBRARY, UNITED NATIONS HEADQUARTERS, NEW YORK CITY. *Architects*: Harrison, Abramovitz & Harris. *Artist*: Fritz Glarner, American, abstract mural, 11' 4" x 22'; 1962. *Photograph*: Courtesy of United Nations.

MEDITATION ROOM, UNITED NATIONS HEADQUARTERS, NEW YORK CITY. *Architects*: International team of fourteen consultants; director of planning, Wallace K. Harrison; deputy director of planning, Max Abramovitz. *Artist*: Bo Beskow, Swedish, fresco in blue, white, gray, and yellow, 9' high x 6½' wide; 1957. *Photograph*: Courtesy of United Nations.

GENERAL ASSEMBLY BUILDING, UNITED NATIONS HEAD-
QUARTERS, NEW YORK CITY. *Architects*: International team of
fourteen consultants; director of planning, Wallace K. Harrison;
deputy director of planning, Max Abramovitz. *Artist*: Candido
Portinari, Brazilian, "War," mural, oil on cedar plywood, 34' x 46';
1957. *Photograph*: Courtesy of United Nations.

SECURITY COUNCIL CHAMBER, UNITED NATIONS HEAD-
QUARTERS, NEW YORK CITY. *Architects*: International team of
fourteen consultants; director of planning, Wallace K. Harrison;
deputy director of planning, Max Abramovitz; chamber designer,
Arnstein Arneberg, Norwegian. *Artist*: Per Krogh, Norwegian,
"Emergence from War and Slavery to Freedom," mural, 25' wide
x 20' high; 1966. *Photograph*: Courtesy of United Nations.

LOBBY, SECRETARIAT BUILDING, UNITED NATIONS HEADQUARTERS, NEW YORK CITY. *Architects*: International team of fourteen consultants; director of planning, Wallace K. Harrison; deputy director of planning, Max Abramovitz. *Artist*: Marc Chagall, French, stained-glass panel, 12' x 18'; theme, "Peace and Man"; 1964. *Photograph*: Courtesy of United Nations.

DAG HAMMARSKJOLD LIBRARY, UNITED NATIONS HEADQUARTERS, NEW YORK CITY. *Architects*: Harrison, Abramovitz & Harris. *Artist*: Bo Beskow, Swedish, "Composition for a Concave Wall," 14' x 26'; 1961. *Photograph*: Courtesy of United Nations.

MAIN LOBBY, GENERAL ASSEMBLY BUILDING, UNITED NATIONS HEADQUARTERS, NEW YORK CITY. *Architect*: International team of fourteen consultants; director of planning, Wallace K. Harrison; deputy director of planning, Max Abramovitz. *Art*: Plaster replica of Greek statue, "Poseidon of Artemision," presented by Greek government, 6' 7"; 1953. *Photograph*: Courtesy of United Nations.

INTERNATIONAL SCULPTURE SYMPOSIUM
Long Beach State College, Long Beach, California

An event of extraordinary importance for the encouragement of the arts in the United States occurred in the summer of 1965 on the campus of Long Beach State College (LBSC) in southern California. The director of the First International Sculpture Symposium to be held in the United States was Kenneth Glenn, professor of art at LBSC; the consulting architect was Edward Killingsworth.

Eight sculptors from various countries, including two from the United States, who had been invited to come to the college, devoted their summer months to designing and constructing on the campus grounds eight monumental works, which remained college property.

The purpose of the symposium was to bring the artists together and to give them absolute freedom to create works on assigned campus locations which would express modern technological influences in the United States.

The most heartening factor was the response of the entire community, not only the art patrons but the leaders of industry. More than seventy industries cooperated with the sculptors by supplying materials and facilities with a view to exploring new uses of materials. The sculptors were encouraged to use materials identified with the region. The artists worked in redwood, concrete, and metals such as aluminum, titanium, and stainless steel.

The results achieved by this symposium were manifold. It brought to one place a collection of monumental outdoor sculptures by renowned, internationally recognized artists; it set a precedent for similar symposiums in this country; it served as a catalyst in the promotion of the integration of art and architecture; and it revealed the yet-unexplored possibilities of the "marriage" of technology and art. The symposium should also serve as a tangible symbol of cultural exchange between nations.

The participating sculptors were Gabriel Kohn of Sarasota, Florida; André Bloc of France; Kosso Eloul of Israel; Kengiro Azuma of Japan; Piotr Kowalski, formerly of Poland; J. J. Beljon of the Netherlands; Robert Murray of Canada; Claire Falkenstein of Oregon; and Rita Letendre, muralist of Israel.

Assisting the sculptors were thirty-two students and graduates selected from all parts of the United States. The expectation was that participation in the symposium would provide the students with practical experience in handling materials for work on a monumental scale and would inspire them to great efforts.

INTERNATIONAL SCULPTURE SYMPOSIUM, CAMPUS, CALIFORNIA STATE COLLEGE, LONG BEACH, CALIFORNIA. *Artist*: J. J. Beljon, "Homage to Sam Rodia," painted concrete, 130' long x 3 to 13' high x 25' deep, in nineteen segments; 1965. *Photographer*: Phil Baskin.

INTERNATIONAL SCULPTURE SYMPOSIUM, CAMPUS, CALIFORNIA STATE COLLEGE, LONG BEACH, CALIFORNIA. *Artist*: Robert Murray, "Duet," 1"-thick steel, 10' high x 18' long x 4' wide, weighing 7,000 pounds; 1965. *Photograph*: Courtesy of California State College.

INTERNATIONAL SCULPTURE SYMPOSIUM, CAMPUS, CALIFORNIA STATE COLLEGE, LONG BEACH, CALIFORNIA. *Artist*: Gabriel Kohn, "Long Beach Contract," laminated redwood, 10' x 7', weighing 700 pounds; 1965. *Photograph*: Courtesy of California State College.

INTERNATIONAL SCULPTURE SYMPOSIUM, CAMPUS, CALIFORNIA STATE COLLEGE, LONG BEACH, CALIFORNIA. *Artist*: Kengiro Azuma, "Mu 464," aluminum, 10' 7" high x 5' wide (base), weighing 3,000 pounds; 1965. *Photograph*: Courtesy of California State College.

INTERNATIONAL SCULPTURE SYMPOSIUM, CAMPUS, CALIFORNIA STATE COLLEGE, LONG BEACH, CALIFORNIA. *Artist*: Piotr Kowalski, "Now," stainless steel, 29' 4" high x 10' wide (base) x 3' high (top); radar screen, 6' wide; each sheet weighing 1,850 pounds; 1965. *Photograph*: Courtesy of California State College.

INTERNATIONAL SCULPTURE SYMPOSIUM, CAMPUS, CALIFORNIA STATE COLLEGE, LONG BEACH, CALIFORNIA. *Artist*: Kosso Eloul, "Hardfact," concrete and stainless steel, 21' high x 135' long x 15' wide; 1965. *Photograph*: Courtesy of California State College.

INTERNATIONAL SCULPTURE SYMPOSIUM, CAMPUS, CALI-FORNIA STATE COLLEGE, LONG BEACH, CALIFORNIA. *Artist*: Rita Letendre, "Sunforces," painted mural, black, yellow, and green epoxy paint, 24' x 21'; 1965. *Photograph*: Courtesy of California State College.

Unlike the ornateness of the baroque period, there is an openness, a directness in our lives. We are like skeletons with our backbones exposed. There are questions in the work, too, a searching and questing, just as we ourselves don't have all the answers. . . . Sculpture is a way to communicate. Man is born alone and dies alone. Even with warm friends and a beloved family, he lives alone. But complete loneliness is unbearable and that is good enough reason to communicate. This will draw kindred souls, just as I have seen work done 5,000 years ago and have known at once the artist was my kin. . . . I am not interested in making a decoration. . . . I want an aliveness, an awareness in the reaction it evokes, even if the person doesn't understand his feelings.

Kosso Eloul

I am interested in advanced electronics. . . . I sculpture with machines. . . . I want pedestrians' view in the center of social life, not to be seen by car traffic. . . . With the electro-forming process for metal there is no limit to the force that can be applied because the water absorbs the shock of the explosion. . . . My sculpture is a summing up of what I want to say; I can never speak of it in words.

Piotr Kowalski

This sculpture is one of my best. In its straight clean lines, I have tried to show my ideas as clearly and simply as possible. I don't want unnecessary elements standing in the way. . . . I like to work with industry because American industry is known for its machinery, craftsmanship and techniques. . . . I suppose my self-supporting sculpture is not much different from totem poles. The natives who created them were making a sort of magic, and if my works are objects of mystery I shall be satisfied. . . . My sculptures are complex but not complicated. . . . Plates of steel are taken for granted. I want to discover what I can make of them with my hands and with the extension of my hands through industry.

Robert Murray

My piece is an essay in dovetailing two elements. I tried to link up visually the buildings of the campus and the surrounding landscape. At the same time, I set myself the task of creating a screen, hiding the cars on the campus parking lot. A third aim was to mark the main entrance of the college with a "signal."

J. J. Beljon

I see in the forces of my mural a freshness of the moment while it is happening, as pure as it can be, not a reporting of what has happened. It's as though in a moment the wall will be empty again.

. . . I chose the wall over the passageway because I want people walking in and out of my painting. It must not be static—it must be a dynamic with action and interaction that continues in the mind of the spectator.

Rita Letendre

I call my work "Mu" (nothingness—the meeting of opposite or conflicting forces). In it, are represented earth, man and sky—the universal rather than the particular. There is but one man. . . . I want to feel the story of man. . . . Sculpture is form and volume arranged in a certain way, but I want more than that. I want a spiritual quality, a sense of life in a continuous left to right, up and down, elliptical movement with a continuity you can detect from any point.

Kengiro Azuma

My sculpture will hover six or eight inches over a reflecting pool in front of the new faculty building. It will stand before a curtain of water jetting from the pool. . . . People want an image. They compare the fountain to a great wave continuously breaking, gathering and breaking.

Claire Falkenstein

Of Gabriel Kohn, the American historian Robert Goldwater writes:

Kohn's intention is to get away from the restricting human prototype, people erect upon their feet, and instead to "open up things" Kohn creates individual shapes and then puts them together in the spirit of the laboratory chemist, probing balance and imbalance until a stable compound is found.

André Bloc was deeply committed to sculptural architecture as a means of returning contemporary man to a more intimate relationship with his environment:

"Modern architecture" is cold, detrimental to beauty. Our civilization is completely materialistic—dependent on automobiles and machines.

With his sculptural architecture he sought to unite man with his environment in a warmer, more personal relationship:

The world is often ugly. This symposium can be an example of the ways we can lessen the ugliness around us.

Bloc was killed in an accident in India in 1966.

Part II

Countries Around the World

It has been an exciting discovery to receive examples of the collaboration of the arts with architecture from the many countries around the world. It is refreshing to see the excellent use of sculptural concrete forms as part of the structure by Dutch and Mexican sculptors; the monumental welded steel free standing pieces created by German, French and Swiss artists; the extensive use of stained glass not only in churches but in homes and business places; the Sgraffito designs in marble and concrete done in Greece and Spain; the interesting sculptural shapes of buildings such as the Museum of the Book in Jerusalem, churches in France and Switzerland and the Juarez Museum in Mexico; the precast aggregate murals in Central and South American countries. Of much interest are the new shapes of concrete playground sculpture found in several European countries.

In most of the public and civic buildings shown here, the governmental authorities, whether city or federal, supported the art programs. The tradition of support of art projects by private art patrons is disappearing and the government, as in France, is allocating 1% of the construction budget of all public buildings to be used for the fine arts as part of the building.

This book was not intended to cover fully all the countries around the world. Contact was made with the national architectural societies in all countries. They were asked to notify their members through their publications. The most active societies replied and it can be assumed that the countries represented here give a fair cross section of the current state of artist-architect collaboration. There is no doubt, however, that there are many fine artists and architects whose work is not represented. This holds true also for the countries which are not represented here.

CIVIC CENTER, CANBERRA, AUSTRALIA. *Architects*: Yuncken Freeman Architects Pty. Ltd. *Artist*:
Tom Bass, "Ethos," sculpture representing spirit of the community, bronze, 18' high; 1961. *Photographers*: Max Dupain & Associates Pty. Ltd. for National Capital Development Commission.

CIVIC CENTER, CANBERRA, AUSTRALIA. *Architects*: Yuncken Freeman Architects Pty. Ltd. *Artist*: Tom Bass, "Ethos," sculpture representing spirit of the community, bronze, 18' high; 1961. *Photographers*: Max Dupain & Associates Pty. Ltd. for National Capital Development Commission.

CANBERRA THEATER CENTER, CANBERRA, AUSTRALIA. *Architects*: Yuncken Freeman Architects Pty. Ltd. *Artist*: Robert Cook, "Thespis," sculpture of semilegendary Greek dramatic poet of the sixth century B.C., known as Father of Greek Tragedy, 13' long x 9' high; 1965. *Photographer*: Australian News and Information Bureau for the National Capital Development Commission.

ADMINISTRATION AND PRODUCTION CENTERS, SMITH, KLINE & FRENCH LABORATORIES, LIMITED, SYDNEY, AUSTRALIA. *Architects*: Brown, Brewer & Gregory. *Artist*: Leonard Hessing, precast concrete mural with rod and tube inserts of spun concrete and chrome-plated steel, 20' x 10'; completed 1962. *Photographers*: Max Dupain & Associates Pty. Ltd.

B'NAI B'RITH HOUSE, MELBOURNE, AUSTRALIA. *Architect*: Dr. Ernest Fooks. *Artist*: Max Lyle, menorah, copper sculpture, 6' 9" x 8' 6"; 1958. *Photographer*: Wolfgang Sievers.

BANQUE LAMBERT, BRUSSELS, BELGIUM. *Architects*: Skidmore, Owings & Merrill. *Artist*: Henry Moore, "Lambert Locking Piece," bronze, 115½" high; 1965. *Photographers*: Errol Jackson Photography.

CIVIC CENTER, GUATEMALA CITY, GUATEMALA. *Architects*: Jorge Montes Córdova; Raúl Córdova; Carlos Haeussler; Raúl Minondo. *Artists*: Roberto Gonzáles Goyri; Carlos Mérida; Efrain Recinos; Dagoberto Vásquez Castañeda; 1964. *Photographer*: Pablo Sittler.

BANK OF GUATEMALA, GUATEMALA CITY, GUATEMALA. *Architects*: Jorge Montes Córdova; Raúl Minondo. *Artist*: Carlos Mérida; 1964. *Photographer*: Ricardo Mata.

EAST ELEVATION (left), **WEST ELEVATION** (right), **BANK OF GUATEMALA, GUATEMALA CITY, GUATEMALA.** *Architects*: Jorge Montes Córdova; Raúl Córdova; Raúl Minondo. *Artists*: East Elevation, Dagoberto Vásquez Castañeda, deep relief in reinforced concrete, 21' x 120'; west elevation, Roberto Gonzáles Goyri, deep relief in reinforced concrete, 21' x 120'; 1964. *Photographers*: East elevation, Julia Zachrisson; west elevation, Abraham Gutt.

CARRANZA BUILDING, GUATEMALA CITY, GUATEMALA. *Architects*: Holzheu & Holzheu. *Artist*: Dagoberto Vásquez Castañeda, concrete bas-relief mural, cast in place, 570' x 6'; 1962. *Photographer*: Julia Zachrisson.

THEATER, INGOLSTADT/DONAU, WEST GERMANY. *Architect*: Hart-Waltherr Hämer. *Artist*: Hans Aeschbacher, "Figure III, Explorer 2," Carrara-marble sculpture, 12' x 2' x 2'; 1965. *Photographer*: Hans Aeschbacher.

ELECTRIC PLANT, MIRANDA, ASTURIAS, SPAIN. *Architect*: Joaquín Vaquero.
Artist: Joaquín Vaquero, reliefs carved on concrete at entrance to tunnel, 31' 5" x
12'; 1962. *Photographers*: Uria Foto.

Above and Below:
ELECTRIC PLANT, GRANDAS DE SALIME, SPAIN. *Architect*: Joaquín Vaquero. *Artist*: Vaquero Turcios, bas-relief on facade, 69' x 46' 5"; single units, 9' x 9'; 1958. *Photographers*: Pando, Madrid (above); Uria Foto (below).

ELECTRIC PLANT, GRANDAS DE SALIME, SPAIN. *Architect*: Joaquín Vaquero. *Artist*: Vaquero Turcios, murals; left, "Electrical Discharge," 13' 5" x 147'; right, "The Creation of Electrical Energy," 17' 7" x 183'; upper part of wall, "The Four Elements: Electricity, Formulas, Water, and Mechanical Elements"; 1958. *Photographer*: Pando, Madrid.

SEMINARIO EUDISTA DE LEON, SPAIN. *Architect:* Efrem García Fernández. *Artist:* Efrem García Fernández. *Collaborating Artist:* José Pérez Paramio, brick mural relief, 30' high; 1964. *Photograph:* Courtesy of Efrem García Fernández.

SAN PEDRO MARTYR DOMINICAN SEMINARY, MADRID, SPAIN. *Architect*: Miguel Fisac.
Artists: Pablo Serrano, bronze crucifix, 14' high; Adolfo C. Winternitz, stained-glass windows,
27' high, approximately 3,000 square feet; 1960. *Photograph*: Courtesy of Adolfo C. Winternitz.

INTERNATIONAL AIRPORT, PALMA DE MALLORCA, SPAIN. *Architect*: Eduardo Aguirre Basse.
Artist: Vaquero Turcios, steel sculpture, 35' long; 1967. *Photograph*: Courtesy of Vaquero Turcios.

CAVANELAS GARDENS, RIO DE JANEIRO, BRAZIL. *Architect*: Oscar Niemeyer Soares Filho. *Landscape Architect*: Roberto Burle Marx. *Artist*: Alfredo Ceschiati, bronze sculpture; 1954. *Photographer*: Marcel Gautherot.

SAN IGNACIO SCHOOL, SANTIAGO, CHILE. *Architect*: Alberto Piwonka. *Artist*: Mario Carreño, glass mosaic mural, 21' x 81'; 1960. *Photograph*: Courtesy of Mario Carreño.

OLIVO GOMES RESIDENCE, RIO DE JANEIRO, BRAZIL. *Architects*: Rino Levi; Roberto Cerqueira César. *Artist*: Roberto Burle Marx, glazed-tile wall mural and mosaic mural; 1954. *Photographer*: Marcel Gautherot.

VERBO DIVINO CHURCH, SANTIAGO, CHILE. *Architects*: Sergio Larrain; Emilio Duhart; Mario Pérez De Arce; Alberto Piwonka. *Artist*: Adolfo C. Winternitz, stained-glass windows; 1962. *Photographer*: Bob Borowicz, Santiago.

CASINO, VINA DEL MAR, CHILE. *Architect*: Francisco Dominguez Errazuriz. *Artist*: Mario Carreño, mural on three walls, metal plates colored white, black, and ochre with red forms; side walls, 15' x 63', front wall, 12' x 30'; 1961. *Photograph*: Courtesy of Mario Carreño.

CSSR EXPO. '58, BRUSSELS, BELGIUM; NOW AT BRNO, CZECHOSLOVAKIA. *Architects*: F. Cubr; J. Hrubý; Z. Pokorný. *Artist*: Vincenc Makovsky, "The Sun of Socialism," bronze sculpture, 8½' high; 1958. *Photograph*: Courtesy of Josef Hrubý.

CSSR EXPO. '58, BRUSSELS, BELGIUM; NOW AT LATERNA MAGIKA THEATER, PRAGUE, CZECHOSLOVAKIA. *Architects*: F. Cubr; J. Hrubý; Z. Pokorný. *Artist*: Vladimir Janousek, "The Magic Lantern," reinforced concrete, 6' high; 1959. *Photographer*: Frantisek Illek.

GANADERO BANK, POPAYAN, COLOMBIA. *Architect*: Jaime Coronel. *Artist*: Edgar Negret, "Endless Column," red-painted aluminum; 1967. *Photograph*: Courtesy of Edgar Negret.

STATE LIBRARY, ARHUS UNIVERSITY, ARHUS, DENMARK. *Architect*: C. F. Moller. *Artist*: Morten Nielsen, wood sculptured figures, 6' high; theme, "Past, Present, Future of Science"; 1963. *Photographers*: Hammerschmidt Foto Arhus.

PALAIS DU SENAT, TEHERAN, IRAN. *Architects*: Foroughi & Chiai. *Artist*: André Bloc, metal columns, 75' high; 1961. *Photographer*: Thomas Gugini.

For a number of years I have studied the relationship between art and architecture.

About eight years ago I was commissioned by the architects in charge of the construction of the Palais du Senat in Teheran to realize two important sculptures which added to the monumentality of the official building for which I used a certain sheet-iron technique to support the reinforced concrete.

There are two positions that one may take in a situation of this kind—form the works of art in complete independence, without any rapport to the architectural problem, or in complete rapport, therefore complementing, as much as possible, the work of the sculptor and that of the architect. I adopted the latter. It seemed to me that, because of the exceptional dimensions of the sculptures to be realized (75 feet in height) and because of their position in respect to the building, it was difficult to solve the problem in total independence.

André Bloc

MEDICAL CENTER, HARBURG, HAMBURG, WEST GERMANY. *Architects*: Hamburg Municipal Architectural Department for Harburg. *Artist*: Berto Lardera, "Between Two Worlds II," iron and copper, 9' high; 1959. *Photographer*: Berto Lardera.

Architecture consists of an organized relationship between interior and exterior spaces, conditioned by a definite function. This function creates the material conditions necessary to any architectural structure. Sculpture is a free spatial structure, defining and containing space, conditioned only by a vitality of its expression. The impulse to sculpture is the interior necessity of this expression.

In my opinion, the relation between sculpture and architecture is possible only if they both keep their full individuality. In its relation to architecture, sculpture should in no case renounce its own specific qualities, nor should architecture, of course, in its relation to sculpture.

In town planning the aim of the sculpture should consist in creating a connection and a unity among the different architectures and the elements of the town planning and imposing to the functional forms an entirely free expression. Through this imposition a new vitality can arise. The creation of an articulated, wider space, a space in which human beings live and act, may become a new aim in art. Through this new attitude and after such a long period of separation between art and the public, art would no longer be a field reserved to the limited number of art lovers, but would become a real necessity to everybody. The adventure of single individuals, architects, painters and sculptors, may then become the adventure of the man in the street. Art would then be the expression of an entire society, as it was in the high epochs of antiquity.

Berto Lardera

Above and Right:
FOYER, MUNICIPAL THEATER, FRANKFURT AM MAIN, WEST GERMANY. *Architects*: Apel & Beckert. *Artist*: Zoltan Kemeny, spatial sculpture in brass, 30' high x 360' long; 1963. *Photographers*: Foto Ursula Seitz-Gray.

A mural relief which shows the movement of man in his aspiration suggests even higher goals. Prof. Naegeli introduced me into the life of the school and showed me the aims. The combination of these two contacts, the architect and the professor, gave the balance to our collaboration. This enabled me to create my mural relief, which has become an organic part of the school; of its architecture and of its spirit of education. . . . I have tried to conceive a work which captures the interest of the students, who are free to imagine plans of multiple cities in which they are able to make their own integration.

Zoltan Kemeny

Opposite:
FOYER, MUNICIPAL THEATER, FRANKFURT AM MAIN, WEST GERMANY. *Architects*: Apel & Beckert. *Artist*: Zoltan Kemeny, spatial sculpture in brass, 30' high x 360' long; 1963. *Photographers*: Foto Ursula Seitz-Gray.

PUBLIC HIGH SCHOOL, COLOGNE, WEST GERMANY. *Architects*: Franz Lammersen and Franz Löwenstein, Cologne Building Department. *Artist*: Arnaldo Pomodoro, bronze and cement bas-relief, 78' 6" x 26' 3"; 1964. *Photographer*: Ugo Mulas. *Photograph*: Courtesy of Marlborough-Gerson Gallery, Inc., New York.

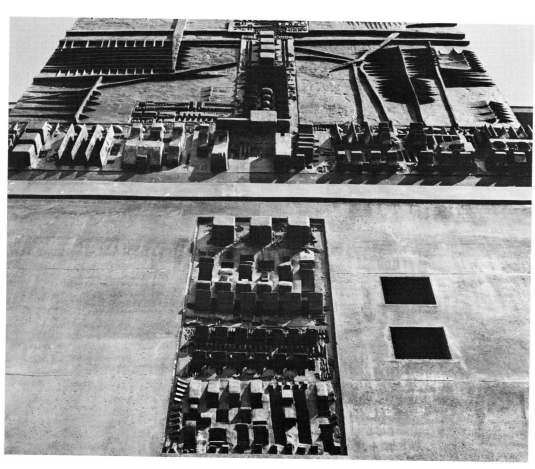

ST. STEPHEN CATHOLIC CHURCH, ARLEN, WEST GER-
MANY. *Architect*: Dr. Justus Dahinden; 1966. *Photographer*:
Michael Wolgensinger.

V. LANGEN RESIDENCE, MEERERBUSCH, NEAR DUSSELDORF, WEST GERMANY.
Architect: Lüneborg. *Artist*: Berto Lardera, "The Hours and The Days I," metal
sculpture, 12' x 12'; 1959. *Photographer*: Berto Lardera.

Above and Below:
SCHOOL, EGER, HUNGARY. *Architect*: L. Mányoki. *Artist*: T. Vilt, stone relief, 18' x 27'; 1961. *Photograph*: Courtesy of Union of Hungarian Architects.

CUSTOMHOUSE, HEGYESHALOM, HUNGARY. *Architect*: R. Hont. *Artist*: I. Varga, white limestone sculpture, 9'; 1965. *Photograph*: Courtesy of Union of Hungarian Architects.

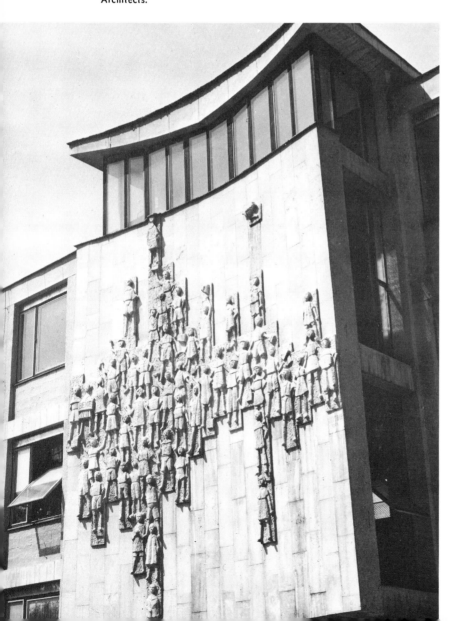

SZOT, HUNGARIAN TRADES UNION COUNCIL HEADQUARTERS, MISKOLC, HUNGARY. *Architect*:
A. Vass. *Artist*: S. Kiss, bronze sculpture, cast stone fitted with iron, quarry stone, 6' 6"; 1962. *Photo-graph*: Courtesy of Union of Hungarian Architects.

APARTMENT BUILDING, SZEGED, HUNGARY. *Architect*: B. Borvendég. *Artist*:
A. Makrisz, bronze sculpture, 6' x 6'; 1961. *Photograph*: Courtesy of Union of Hungarian Architects.

FILM LABORATORY, BUDAPEST, HUNGARY. *Architects*: Kondorai & Vajna.
Artist: S. Kiss, ceramic mural, 12' x 9'; 1962. *Photograph*: Courtesy of Union of Hungarian Architects.

JESUS OBRERO PARISH CHURCH, LIMA, PERU. *Architects*: Haaker & Veloachaga. *Artist*: Adolfo C. Winternitz, mural, 1,500 square feet; stained-glass windows, 150 square feet; 1963. *Photographers*: Casals' Studio.

ST. ROSA DE LIMA PARISH CHURCH OF MARYKNOLL FATHERS, LIMA, PERU. *Architect*: Ricardo Sarria S. *Artist*: Adolfo C. Winternitz, fourteen stained-glass windows, 21' 4" to 31' 2" high x 4' wide; 1960. *Photographers*: Casals' Studio.

CATHEDRAL OF COV-
ENTRY, COVENTRY,
ENGLAND. *Architect*:
Sir Basil Spence. *Artists*:
Sir Jacob Epstein, "St.
Michael and the Devil,"
bronze, 25' high; Law-
rence Lee, Geoffrey
Clarke, and Keith New,
ten stained-glass win-
dows, each 70' high;
1962. *Photographers*: P.
W. and L. Thompson.
Photograph: Courtesy of
provost and chapter of
Coventry.

CATHEDRAL OF COVENTRY, COVENTRY, ENGLAND. *Architect*: Sir Basil
Spence. *Artist*: Sir Jacob Epstein, "St. Michael and the Devil," bronze; 1962.
Photographers: P. W. and L. Thompson.

TIME/LIFE BUILDING, LONDON, ENGLAND. *Architect*: Michael Rosenauer.
Artist: Henry Moore, "Time/Life Screen," Portland stone, 26' 6" x 10'; 1953.
Interior Designers: Sir Hugh Casson and Misha Black. *Photographers*: Errol
Jackson Photography.

COOPERATIVE INSURANCE SOCIETY HEADQUARTERS, MANCHESTER, ENGLAND. *Architect:* G. S. Hay. *Consulting Architect:* Sir John Burnet, Tait & Partners. *Interior Designers:* Design Research Unit, Partners in charge, Misha Black and Alexander Gibson. *Artist:* George Mitchell, mural cast fiberglass panels with aluminum finish, 30' long; 1962. *Photographer:* John Maltby.

SOUTHEND-ON-SEA CIVIC CENTER, ESSEX, ENGLAND. *Architect:* Patrick Burridge. *Artist:* Don Foster, bronze doors, 13' x 11' 4"; design based on the thirty-two alphabet letters in Southend-on-Sea—per-Mare-per-Ecclesia; 1966. *Photographer:* James Frederick Rimmer.

THE ROYAL GARDEN HOTEL, KENSINGTON, LONDON, ENGLAND. *Architects*: R. Siefert & Associates. *Interior Design*: Design Research Unit; Misha Black and Kenneth Bayes. *Artist*: Leonard Rosoman, "Aerial Figures," ceiling, 60' long; 1965. *Photographer*: Colin Westwood.

THE ROYAL GARDEN HOTEL, KENSINGTON, LONDON, ENGLAND. *Architects*: R. Siefert & Associates. *Interior Design*: Design Research Unit; Misha Black and Kenneth Bayes. *Artist*: David Partridge, "Galaxy," recessed ceiling, 14' x 9' 4½", constructed of nails hammered into timber panels, each 3' 8" x 4' 8"; 1965. *Photographer*: Colin Westwood.

Apparent now is the new approach of Mexican architects in designing government buildings. No longer are the architects interested in, or does the government insist on, historical murals or bas-reliefs to decorate public buildings. The tradition of the decorative style of the pyramids has spent itself on the university and other previously erected government buildings. A more subdued and sophisticated approach is now being taken by the architects. This new approach is welcomed by young painters and sculptors, who oppose purely representational forms and who want to create art which expresses contemporary life.

The most dramatic building in Mexico City today is the National Museum of Anthropology, designed by architects Pedro Ramírez Vázquez, Rafael Mijares A., and Jorge Campuzano. It is excellently located in Chapultepec Park, and the entire concept is a fine example of the integration of the arts with the architecture and with the landscaped surroundings. The exterior walls are simple surfaces of native materials. The focal point is the interior court, which includes a monumental fountain by sculptor Morado and a reflecting pool. The area around the pool is designed for several permanent sculptured pieces. The sloping topography is utilized for broad terraced stairs, which lead to lower plazas and open-air restaurants and gardens.

The interior exhibits depicting the history of Mexico are considered the best designed in the world. Here, permanent murals are used sparingly. The mural by Tamayo is the highlight of the main lobby.

Another good example of the new Mexican architecture is the Juárez Museum in Juárez, designed by architects Vázquez, Mijares, and Graf. The geometrically shaped forms of the building express both sculptural and architectural qualities. Here again, the exterior wall surfaces are kept simple and unadorned.

JUAREZ MUSEUM, JUAREZ, MEXICO. *Architects*: Pedro Ramírez Vázquez; Rafael Mijares A.; Eduardo Graf; 1963. *Photographer*: Armando Salas Portugal.

ENTRANCE TO URBAN DEVELOPMENT, JARDINES DEL BOSQUE, GUADALAJARA, MEXICO. *Landscape Architect:* Luis Barragan. *Artist:* Mathias Goeritz, "Yellow Bird," sculpture; 1957. *Photographer:* Marianne Goeritz.

FEDERAL DISTRICT PENITEN- TIARY, MEXICO CITY, MEXICO. *Architect:* Ramón Marcos. *Artist:* Arnold Belkin, "We Are All Guilty," mural, 10' x 75'; 1961. *Photograph:* Courtesy of Arnold Belkin.

SPORT CENTER, DEPORTIVO BA- HIA, MEXICO CITY, MEXICO. *Artist:* Manuel Felguerez, mural of mother-of-pearl, abalone, and oy- ster shells, 300' x 15'; 1963. *Pho- tographer:* Manuel Felguerez.

NATIONAL MUSEUM OF ANTHROPOLOGY, MEXICO CITY, MEXICO. *Architects*: Pedro Ramírez Vázquez; Rafael Mijares A.; Jorge Campuzano. *Artists*: José Chávez Morado, bronze bas-relief column for fountain, 70' (above); Rafael Tamayo, mural, 10' x 20' (below); 1964. *Photographer*: A. Diaz.

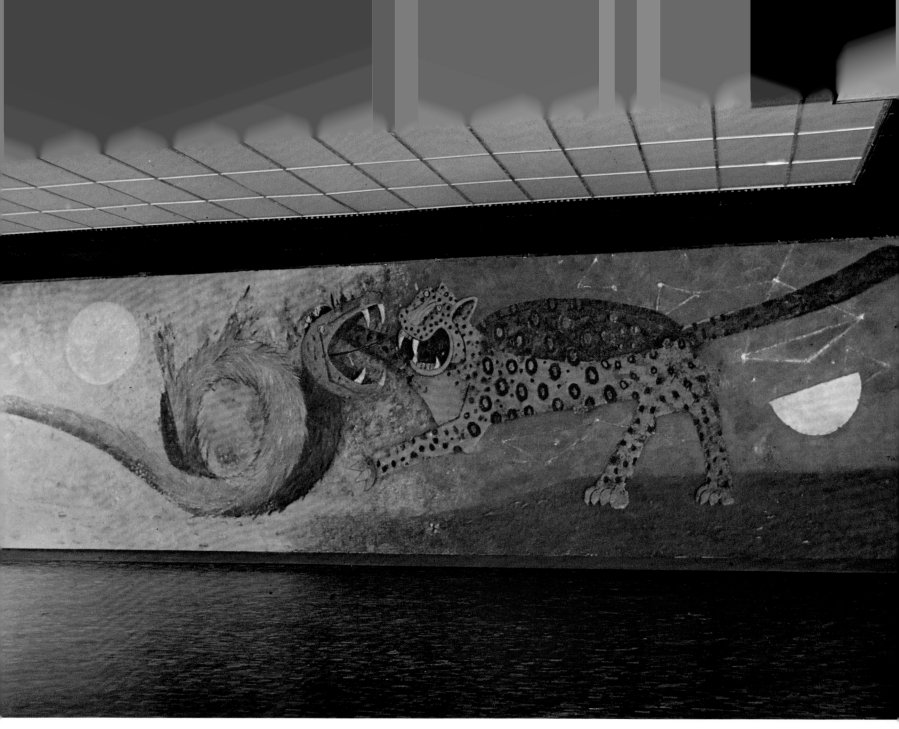

NATIONAL MUSEUM OF ANTHROPOLOGY, MEXICO CITY, MEXICO. *Architects*: Pedro Ramírez Vázquez; Rafael Mijares A.; Jorge Campuzano. *Artist*: Rafael Tamayo, mural, 10' x 20'; 1964. *Photograph*: Courtesy of Pedro Ramírez Vázquez.

GABRIEL O. SAABEDRA RESIDENCE, PEDREGAL SECTION, MEXICO CITY, MEXICO. *Architect*: Leopoldo Gout. *Artist*: Manuel Felguerez, welded-metal and stained-glass-window mural, 20' x 6'; 1965. *Photographer*: Louis G. Redstone.

CONFEDERACION DE CAMARAS INDUSTRIALES BUILDING, MEXICO CITY, MEXICO. *Architect*: Leopoldo Gout. *Artist*: Manuel Felguerez, metal mural, 24' x 12'; 1964. *Photographer*: Louis G. Redstone.

JEWISH COMMUNITY CENTER, MEXICO CITY, MEXICO. *Architect*: Pascual Broid. *Artist*: Arnold Belkin, mural, 150' x 22'; 1966. *Photograph*: Courtesy of Arnold Belkin.

NATIONAL MUSEUM OF ANTHROPOLOGY, MEXICO CITY, MEXICO. *Architects*: Pedro Ramírez Vázquez; Rafael Mijares A.; Jorge Campuzano. *Artist*: José Chávez Morado, bronze bas-relief column for fountain, 70'; 1964. *Photographer*: A. Diaz.

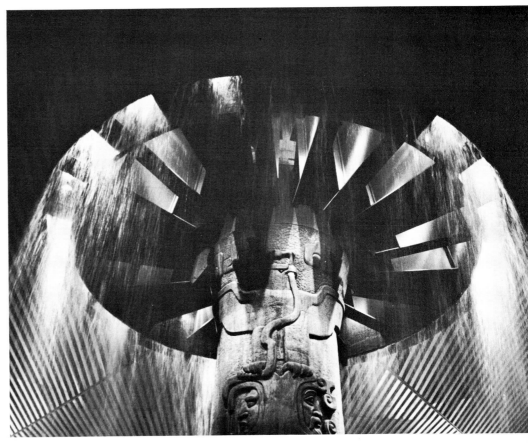

AUTOMEX, TOLUCA, MEXICO.
Architects: Ricardo Legorreta V. Arquitectos; Carlos Hernández; Ramiro Alatorre; Noe Castro Castro. *Artist*: Mathias Goeritz, sculptural landmark, painted concrete, 150' high; 1964. *Photographers*: Cia. Mexicana Aerofoto, S.A.

STATE CAPITOL BUILDING, CAMPECHE, MEXICO. *Architect*: Joaquin Alvarez Ordóñez. *Artist*: José Chávez Morado, mural facade (not shown); 1963. *Photographers*: Foto Cine Colon-Vernis, S.A.

SMITH, KLINE & FRENCH LABORATORIES, LTD., MEXICO CITY, MEXICO. *Architects*: Ricardo Legoretta V. Arquitectos; Carlos Hernández; Ramiro Alatorre; Noe Castro Castro. *Artist*: Mathias Goeritz, iron grill, 159′ long x 11′ 6″ high; 1965. *Photographer*: Kati Horna.

AUDITORIUM, NATIONAL BANK (CREDITO AGRICOLA), MEXICO CITY, MEXICO. *Architects*: Consultas, Investigaciones, Estudios, Proyectos y Supervisión, Sociedad Civil, Ingenieros Consultores Proyectistas. *Artist*: Roberto Berdecio, "Ancient Gods of Agriculture," mural, 10′ x 27′; 1964. *Photographer*: Eric Schwarz.

MUSEUM, CHAPULTEPEC PARK, MEXICO CITY, MEXICO. *Architect*: Pedro Ramírez Vázquez. *Artist*:
José Chávez Morado, bronze doors, 36′ x 9′ 6″; 1960. *Photograph*: Courtesy of Pedro Ramírez Vázquez.

LOBBY, ELKEMBYGGET BUILDING, OSLO, NORWAY. *Architect*: Erling Viksjo.
Artist: Odd Tandberg, silicon mural screen wall; 1965. *Photographer*: Enerett.

NORDSETER CHURCH, LILLEHAMMER, NORWAY. *Architect*:
Erling Viksjo. *Artist*: Odd Tandberg, "metal concrete" panels,
3' x 3'; 1965. *Photographers*: Holst Studio.

SHRINE OF THE BOOK, ISRAEL MUSEUM, JERUSALEM, ISRAEL. *Architects*: Frederick J. Kiesler;
Armand Bartos; 1965. *Photographers*: David Harris (above); David Rubinger (below).

SHRINE OF THE BOOK, ISRAEL MUSEUM, JERUSALEM, ISRAEL. *Architects:* Frederick J. Kiesler; Armand Bartos; 1965. *Photographer:* W. Braun.

BILLY ROSE ART GARDEN, ISRAEL ART MUSEUM, JERUSALEM, ISRAEL. *Architects:* Prof. A. L. Mansfeld; Devora Gad. *Landscape Architect-Artist:* Isamu Noguchi. *Artists:* (from right to left) Auguste Rodin, "Balzac," bronze; Isamu Noguchi, "Khmer"; Germaine Richier, "Le Grand Diabolo"; Reg Butler, "Young Girl with Chemise"; Alberto Viani, "The Girl Friend"; José de Creeft, "Woman in the Sun"; 1965. *Photographer:* Keren-Or.

KIRYAT YAM, ISRAEL. *Architect*: Arie Sharon. *Artist*: Ygael Tumarkin, wall, 60' x 18' x 7'; 1964. *Photographer*: Ygael Tumarkin.

Above and Below:
CENTER B, ASHDOD, ISRAEL: *Artist*: Ygael Tumarkin, stainless steel sculpture, 25' high; 1965. *Photographer*: Ygael Tumarkin.

RECEPTION HALL, KNESSET (PARLIAMENT) BUILDING, JERUSALEM, ISRAEL. *Architects*: Joseph Klarvein; interior, Devora Gad, Arjeh L. Noy. *Artist*: Moshe Elezar Castel, "Glory to Jerusalem," mural, red and black-gray crushed basalt, 23' x 10'; 1966. *Photographer*: Aharon Donagi.

YAD VASHEM (MEMORIAL TO THE SIX MILLION JEWS), JERUSALEM, ISRAEL. *Architect*: Arjeh El-Hanani. *Artist*: David Palombo and B. Shatz, bronze doors; 1961. *Photographer*: Louis G. Redstone.

"THE HALLS OF THE NATION," CONVENTION HALL, JERUSALEM, ISRAEL. *Architects*: Rechter, Zarchi, Rechter. *Artist*: Yaacov Agam, ceiling mural; 1962. *Photographer*: Aharon Donagi.

THE ATHENS HILTON HOTEL, ATHENS, GREECE. *Architects*: Pr. Vassiliades; E. Vourekas; S. Staikos. *Artist*: Yannis Moralis, linear composition in marble, 48' x 117'; 1962. *Photograph*: Courtesy of Yannis Moralis.

DIONYSUS RESTAURANT, PHILOPPAPPOS, GREECE. *Architects*: Pr. Vassiliades; E. Vourekas; S. Staikos. *Artist*: Yannis Moralis, mosaic paving in plaza, 28' 5" x 28' 5"; 1962. *Photograph*: Courtesy of Yannis Moralis.

TRAVELER'S COLUMN, SPOLETO, ITALY. *Artist:* Arnaldo Pomodoro, bronze column, 102' x 17'; 1965. *Photographer:* Ugo Mulas. *Photograph:* Courtesy of Marlborough-Gerson Gallery, Inc., New York.

ST. PETER'S BASILICA, VATICAN, ROME, ITALY.
Artist: Giacomo Manzù, "Porta della Morte," bronze
doors, 23' x 11'; 1964. *Photographers*: Foto Ross.

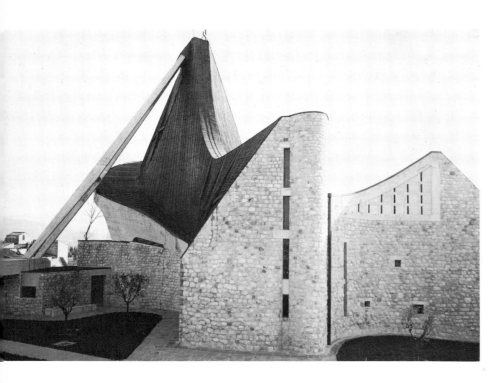

THE CHURCH OF THE MOTORWAY TO THE SUN, FLOR-
ENCE, ITALY. *Architect*: Giovanni Michelucci. *Artist*: Emilio
Greco, "Patron Saints" in east part of the Nave, bronze, 8'
high; 1964. *Photographer*: Gaio Bacci.

NEW UNDERGROUND ADDITION, UNESCO BUILDING, PARIS, FRANCE. *Architect*: Bernard H. Zehrfuss. *Associate Architect*: Marcel Faure. *Artist*: De Swoboda, mosaic paving, 1965 (above); Henry Moore, sculpture at ground level, relocated 1965 (below). *Photograph*: Courtesy of Bernard H. Zehrfuss.

Above:
UNESCO BUILDING, PARIS, FRANCE. *Architects*: Pier Luigi Nervi in collaboration with Marcel Breuer and Bernard H. Zehrfuss. *Artist*: Henry Moore, "Reclining Figure," sculpture; relocated 1965. *Photographer*: UNESCO/Léon Coirier.

APARTMENT HOUSING, MARLY,
FRANCE. *Architects*: M. M. Marcel
Lods et Beuffé. *Artist*: André Bloc,
pool sculpture, stainless-steel tubes
with red and yellow copper, 13 meters
high; 1960. *Photographer*: Etienne
Bertrand Weill.

POINT DU JOUR, BOIS DE BOULOGNE, PARIS, FRANCE. *Landscape Architect*: Daniel Colin. *Artist*:
François Stahly, sculptured fountain in bronze and stone, 21' high; pool, 42' x 48'; 1965. *Photographers*:
Laurent Pinsard (above); Leni Iselin (below).

CHILDREN'S PLAYGROUND, APARTMENT COMPLEX, L'HAY-LES-ROSES, FRANCE. *Architects*: Lesage, Mahé, Billar. *Artist*: Pierre Szekely, white concrete, 9' high; 1958. *Photographers*: Pierre Joly— Véra Cardot.

APARTMENT COMPLEX, VAUCRESSON, FRANCE. *Architects*: Henri Pottier; J.
Tessier. *Artist*: Pierre Szekely, colored-concrete playground sculpture, 30' x 30' per
group; 1961. *Photographer*: Yves Benard.

APARTMENT COMPLEX, VAUCRESSON, FRANCE. *Architects*: Henri Pottier; J. Tessier. *Artist*: Pierre Szekely, colored-concrete playground sculpture, 30' x 30' per group; 1961. *Photographer*: Yves Benard.

APARTMENT HOUSING, CITE D'HABITATION DE L'ELECTRICITE DE FRANCE, CHAMPAGNES/OISE, FRANCE. *Architect*: Jean Fayeton. *Artists*: Pierre Szekely, concrete playground sculpture, 12' high; Vera Szekely, mosaics, 24'; 1961. *Photographers*: Pierre Joly—Véra Cardot.

Above and Below:
CHURCH OF CARMEL DE VALENCIENNES, ST. SAULVE (NORD), FRANCE. *Architects:* Pierre Szekely and Claude Guislain. *Artist:* Pierre Szekely, concrete altar (above), indented concrete design (below); 1966. *Photographers:* Pierre Joly—Véra Cardot.

Above and Below:
CHURCH OF CARMEL DE VALENCIENNES, ST. SAULVE (NORD), FRANCE.
Architects: Pierre Szekely and Claude Guislain. *Artist:* Pierre Szekely, concrete altar (above), indented concrete design (below); 1966. *Photographers:* Pierre Joly— Véra Cardot.

FRENCH TECHNICAL CENTER, LE MANS, FRANCE.
Architect: Pierre Vago. *Artist:* Berto Lardera, "Between Two Worlds IV," iron and stainless-steel sculpture, 13' x 9'; 1964. *Photographer:* Berto Lardera.

Where is modern sculpture going?

This is what all the sculptors are asking themselves; some of them think they are answering this question by doing work which performs practically the same roles as painting and they are providing the collectors, the museums and the art critics with "object-sculptures" which are three-dimensional paintings. These "object-sculptures" can't, certainly, constitute the main activity of the sculptor.

Our world, as permeated as it is by poetic elements, still needs the help of all its artists to realize an environment worthy of the human race. But blinded by the extraordinary progress of technics, our contemporaries think they have opened the doors to a great civilization. They are mistaken. If science and technology are not dominated by a great culture, they can lead us to the worst disaster, not only the cataclysms of war but also the breakup of a very old culture acquired over the centuries.

All the countries colonized during those centuries have seen the disappearance of their cultures, of everything characterizing their way of life, which means primarily their art values. The colonist, who pretended to a higher civilization, has not been able to replace those values.

But let's come back to the role of sculpture in our world where the indifferent masses have little or no use for the efforts of artists. The artists have the duty to participate directly in everyday life in order to fulfill this role. How could they better do it than by contributing directly to the enrichment of the setting of the everyday life? They must participate in the improvement of an architectural and urbanistic order not only by adding to its works of art but by a direct involvement in the elaboration of new architectural trends.

Many artists have become aware of their role. There are symposiums being organized here and there around the world but these are only ephemeral moments, though needed exchanges of points of view between artists are taking place and important works of art are created. The real answer is an everyday work directed towards architectural creation. This is how the sculptor can play a conclusive role in the world of tomorrow, using all the new means of modern techniques and assuming a position of leadership in a world of technicians.[1]

André Bloc
August, 1965

[1] Reprint courtesy of *Arts & Architecture* magazine, vol. 83, no. 12, p. 7, January, 1967.

GARDEN, ANDRE BLOC RESIDENCE, MEUDON, FRANCE. *Architect:* André Bloc. *Artist:* André Bloc, brick and concrete tower, 80' high; 1966. *Photographers:* Michel Moch Photographs.

GARDEN, ANDRE BLOC RESIDENCE, MEUDON, FRANCE. *Architect*: André Bloc, "Habitat II," brick and concrete structure, 39' x 18' (exterior and interior views); 1965. *Photographer*: Gilles Ehrmann.

TRADE SCHOOL, SCHAFFHAUSEN, SWITZERLAND. *Architects*: R. Bächtold & Baumgartner, Rorschach.
Artist: Erwin Rehmann, "Bronzeplastic VI," bronze sculpture, 6' 5" x 9'; 1965. *Photographer*: A. Leoni.

A real integration of architecture and art is as I think—only possible in the case that the architecture is a work of art.

Architecture is a work of art when all its forms, its measures and proportions, the technical solutions and the materials—in addition to their own function—become the expression of an inner human situation. When also a painter or a sculptor out of the same human situation has to work further on such a wall, court or room, both statements can become an harmonious entity.

It is not easy for a painter or a sculptor to combine a work of art afterwards into architecture in the way that both can become an entity. Very often, he will try it with decorative means and along the way he loses the artistic origin. This kind of decorative art I call "artistic ornament." Creative form must be born from within and must not be imposed from the outside.

Erwin Rehmann

SCHOOL, AARAU, SWITZERLAND. *Architect*: Emil Aeschbach, *Artist*: Erwin Rehmann, bronze wall sculpture, 27' x 4' 5''; 1967. *Photograph*: Courtesy of Erwin Rehmann.

DER GLUEHLAMPENWERKE, AARAU, SWITZERLAND. *Architects*: Richner & Bachmann. *Artist*: Erwin
Rehmann, concrete wall, 9' 2" x 34' 4"; 1962. *Photographer*: A. Leoni.

SCHOOLHOUSE, RIEDENHALDE, ZURICH, SWITZERLAND. *Architects*: Hans Escher; Robert Weilenmann; Roland Gross. *Artist*: Hans Aeschbacher, "Figure V, 1960," Swiss Cristallina-marble sculpture, 5' x 10' x 4'; 1960. *Photograph*: Courtesy of Hans Aeschbacher.

SWIMMING AND SPORT ARENA, MYTHENQUAI, SWITZERLAND. *Architects*: Hans & Annemarie Hubacher; Peter Issler. *Artist*: Werner Zryd, zinc pillar tower which indicates time, wind velocity, and temperature, 32' x 18'; 1955. *Photographers*: F. Engasser Foto/Film.

OFFICE BUILDING, HORGEN, ZURICH, SWITZERLAND. *Architect*: Peter Fluor. *Artist*: Hans Aesch-bacher, "Figure IV, 1960," marble sculpture, 15' high x 4' wide x 4' deep; 1960. *Photograph*: Courtesy of Hans Aeschbacher.

ST-GALL GRADUATE SCHOOL OF ECONOMICS, BUSINESS AND PUBLIC ADMINISTRATION, ST-GALL, SWITZERLAND. *Architects*: W. Forderer, R. Otto et Zwimpfer. *Artist*: Alicia Penalba, twelve sculptures, reinforced concrete, 2' x 13.5'; 1963. *Photographers*: F. Maurer (above); Michel Chilo (below).

RADIO SVIZZERA ITALIANA, LUGANO, SWITZERLAND. *Architects:* Camenzind, Jaggli, Tami. *Artist:* Remo Rossi, freestanding bronze sculpture, 15' high; 1966. *Photographer:* V. Vicaris.

Left and Opposite:
COLLEGE, SCHAFFHAUSEN, SWITZERLAND. *Architects*: Bächtold & Baumgartner, Rorschach. *Artist*: Erwin Rehmann, bronze sculpture hanging in opening of underground parking facility (opening is surrounded by water, and sculpture moves in the wind), 19′ high; 1964. *Photographer*: A. Leoni.

"PALME," ZURICH, SWITZERLAND. *Architects*: Haefeli, Moser, Steiger & Studer. *Artist*: Erwin Rehmann, bronze sculptured fountain, 18' high; 1964. *Photograph*: Courtesy of Erwin Rehmann.

HOUSING DEVELOPMENT FOR THE AGED, TANNEBACH DISTRICT, HORGEN, ZURICH, SWITZERLAND. *Architect*: Peter Fluor. *Artist*: Hans Aeschbacher, "Figure III, 1965," sculptured concrete and steel fountain, 14' high x 9' wide x 7.5' deep; 1966. *Photographer*: Hans Aeschbacher.

FOURTH SWISS OPEN-AIR EXHIBITION OF SCULPTURES, NEAR CONGRESS HOUSE, BIEL, SWITZERLAND. *Architect*: Max Schlup. *Artist*: Hans Aeschbacher, "Figure II, 1966," granite, 12' x 2.5' x 2.5'; 1966. *Photographer*: Hans Aeschbacher.

KLOTEN AIRPORT, ZURICH, SWITZERLAND. *Architect*: Heinrich Oeschger. *Artist*: Hans Aeschbacher, "Figure I, 1964, Explorer I," Swiss Cristallina-marble sculpture, 17.5' x 3' x 3'; 1967. *Photographer*: Dölf Preisig.

STAUFEN COLLEGE, STAUFEN, SWITZERLAND. *Architects*: Lehmann & Spogler & Morf. *Artist*: Erwin Rehmann, concrete relief, 13.5' long, and bronze pillar, 7' high, in recreation hall; 1964. *Photographer*: A. Leoni.

STAUFEN COLLEGE, STAUFEN, SWITZERLAND. *Architects*: Lehmann & Spogler & Morf. *Artist*: Erwin Rehmann, concrete relief vertical, 16.5' high, in staircase; 1964. *Photographer*: A. Leoni.

ELEMENTARY SCHOOL, WEGGIS, SWITZERLAND. *Architect*: Dr. Justus Dahinden; 1963. *Photographer*: Max Hellstern.

Basically I consider architecture as a service to mankind and a contribution to human formation of its environment. Architecture, apart from its practical function alone, should be the very transfiguration of artistic influence, especially on important buildings such as churches and public centers.

Architecture should lead and direct people to a new dynamic community and should initiate latent emotional feelings by its aesthetic means. Above all architecture should provide the sensation of giving a home, comfort and a shelter and therefore will always have to find new volume dimensions. This can only be realized by renouncing the imperative of right angles and implementing the infinite resources of new forms and shapes.

Contemporary architecture identifies itself by a plasticity which provides exterior and interior tensions where light and shade underline a sensation of illusion to architectural forms. It is highly important to fight against the influence of sterile intellectualism and the spreading of rigid tendencies of technology, which is used in both individual buildings and town-planning.

Dr. Justus Dahinden

ST. FRANZISKUS CATHOLIC CHURCH, HUTTWILEN, SWITZERLAND. *Architect*:
Dr. Justus Dahinden; 1966. *Photographer*: Michael Wolgensinger.

ST. PAUL CATHOLIC CHURCH, DIELSDORF, SWITZERLAND. *Architect*: Dr. Justus Dahinden; 1962. *Photographer*: Max Hellstern.

MARIA-KRONUNG CATHOLIC CHURCH, ZURICH, SWITZERLAND. *Architect*: Dr. Justus Dahinden; 1966. *Photographer*: Michael Wolgensinger.

CHRISTIAN CENTER ON THE ZOLLIKERBERG, SWITZERLAND. *Architects*: Hans & Annemarie Hubacher; Peter Issler. *Artist*: Robert Lienhard, bronze doors depicting burning bush, 6' 6" x 9' 6"; 1962. *Photographer*: Peter Grunert-Zurich.

REPUBLICA BUILDING, MONTEVIDEO, URUGUAY. *Architect*: Juan J. Casal Rocco. *Artist*: Lincoln Presno, mural, marble aggregates and lead metal strips, 45′ x 10′ 5″; 1963. *Photographer*: R. Aguerre.

LIVING ROOM, RESIDENCE OF DR. ANTONIO ACHE,
GREEN BEACH, MONTEVIDEO, URUGUAY. *Architect*:
Enrique Anbia. *Artist*: Lincoln Presno, mural, marble
aggregates with copper strips, 8' x 9'; 1965. *Photographer*: R. Aguerre.

APARTMENT HOUSE, BELGRADE, YUGOSLAVIA. *Architect*:
Mihajlo Mitrović. *Photographer*: D. Barlovac.

The most striking aspect of modern town planning is its pronounced ugliness, lack of proportion and imagination. The eye casts about in vain for a pleasant disposition of parks and houses. Nowhere is there a delightful architectural detail, finish, a facade with satisfying propositions, a striking detail of craftsmanship, not to mention artistic vision, a feeling for plastic form, space and colour. Here lies the task of the sculptor.

I try by all means to find a place for the sculptor in modern architecture. Not applied sculpture, but integrated sculpture. There is still a long way to go from now until the moment that the artists together with the architects will realize such an integration. But I am sure it will come. Some of my great colleagues have already done, here and there—in collaboration with understanding architects— things that near the ideal.

J. J. Beljon

SECONDARY SCHOOL, MONSTER, NEAR THE HAGUE, HOLLAND. *Architect:* S. G. van den Akkar. *Artist:* J. J. Beljon, relief in concrete, 30' high; 1965. *Photographer:* Kok Storm.

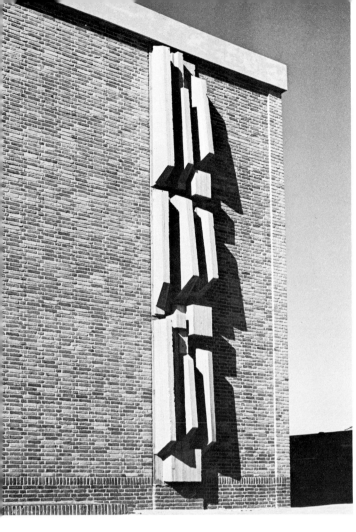

Above and Below:
SECONDARY SCHOOL, MONSTER, NEAR THE HAGUE, HOLLAND. *Architect*: S. G. van den Akkar. *Artist*: J. J. Beljon, relief in concrete, 30' high; 1965. *Photographer*: Kok Storm.

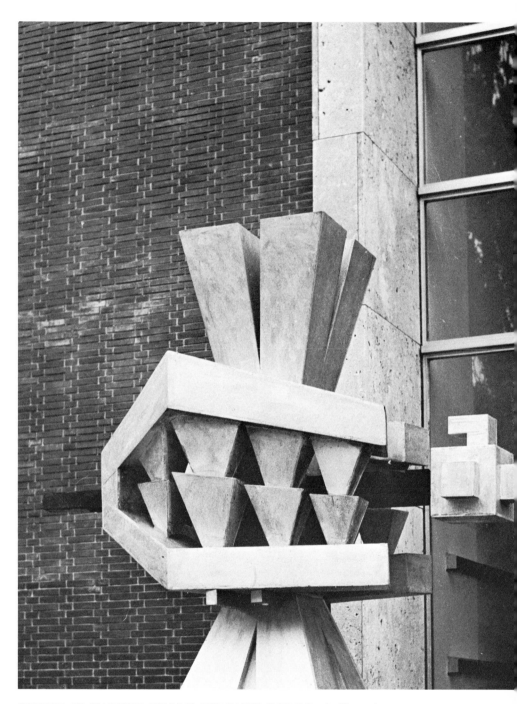

CHAMBER OF COMMERCE BUILDING, THE HAGUE, HOLLAND. *Architect*: Jan Wils. *Artist*: J. J. Beljon, "New Bird," zinc sculpture, 9' high; 1963. *Photographer*: J. J. Beljon.

THE BOUWCENTRUM WALL, BOUWCENTRUM, ROT-
TERDAM, HOLLAND. *Architect*: J. W. C. Boks. *Artist*:
Henry Moore, bas-relief in brick, 28′ 3″ high x 63′ long;
1955. *Photograph*: Courtesy of Henry Moore.

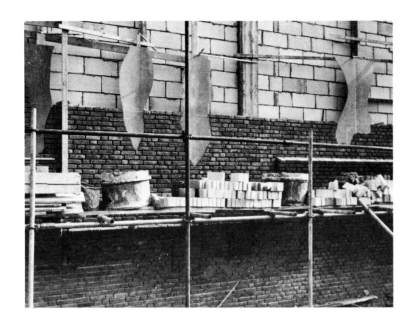

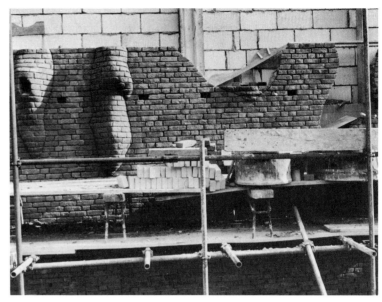

THE BOUWCENTRUM WALL, BOUWCENTRUM, ROTTERDAM, HOLLAND. *Architect*: J. W. C. Boks. *Artist*: Henry Moore, bas-relief in brick, 28′ 3″ high x 63′ long, work in progress; 1955. *Photograph*: Courtesy of Henry Moore.

Above and Below right:
POSTCHEQUE-EN GIRODIENST, THE HAGUE, HOLLAND. *Architect*: Van den Broek en Bakema.
Artist: Carel Visser, reinforced-concrete sculpture; 1966. *Photographer*: J. A. Vrijhof.

TOMADO FACTORY, ETTEN-LEUR, HOLLAND. *Architects*: Maaskant, Van Dommelen, Kroos, Ir Senf. *Artist*: Ossip Zadkine, cast aluminum sculptured mural, 4½' x 14'; 1956. *Photographers*: Foto Spies.

TOWN HALL, HULSBERG, HOLLAND. *Architect*: J. van der Pluym. *Artist*: R. Stultiens, steel tower, painted blue, red, black, and white, 27' high; 1965. *Photographers*: Foto Film Flahaye.

ACADEMY OF ARTS, ARNHEM, HOLLAND. *Architect*: Dr. G. Th. Rietveld. *Artist*: André Bolten, iron sculpture, 13' high; 1962. *Photographers*: Ulkoja.

GAK BUILDING, AMSTERDAM, HOLLAND. *Architects*: Merkelbach & Elling; L. Hartsuyker-Curjel & E. Hartsuyker. *Artists*: Carel Visser, copper and steel frame, 10' x 20'; N. Yonk, bronze, 2' 10" high; C. Kneulman, bronze bas-relief, 11' x 3'; 1964. *Photographers*: Ulkoja.

I wanted the open-air gallery to act as a focus for the little park in front of the building, as a starting point for a growing collection of sculptures, as a gathering point for the people living in the surroundings and as a meeting place for people and sculpture. As a matter of fact, the open-air gallery lived up to the expectation, and beyond! On fair days, young and old sit between and on the sculptures, living and playing with and on them; at lunch-time it is a rest-place for the workers in the great building.

E. Hartsuyker, architect

KROLLER-MULLER MUSEUM, OTTERLO, HOLLAND. *Architect*: Henri van de Velde. *Artist*: Alicia Penalba, mural relief in gold polyester with gold leaf, 12' x 45'; sixteen elements, each 4½' x 8"; 1965. *Photographer*: Michel Chilo.

Below:
ENTRANCE TO SPORT PARK, OOKMEER, AMSTERDAM, HOLLAND. *Architect*: T. Constant Nieuwenhuijs. *Artist*: T. Constant Nieuwenhuijs, concrete, 12' wide x 42' high; 1964. *Photographers*: Town Planning Department, Public Works Department, Amsterdam, Holland.

POLICE STATION, EINDHOVEN, HOLLAND. *Architect*: J. de Haan. *Artist*: R. Stultiens, iron tower in black, white, and blue, 15' high; 1966. *Photographers*: Foto Film Flahaye.

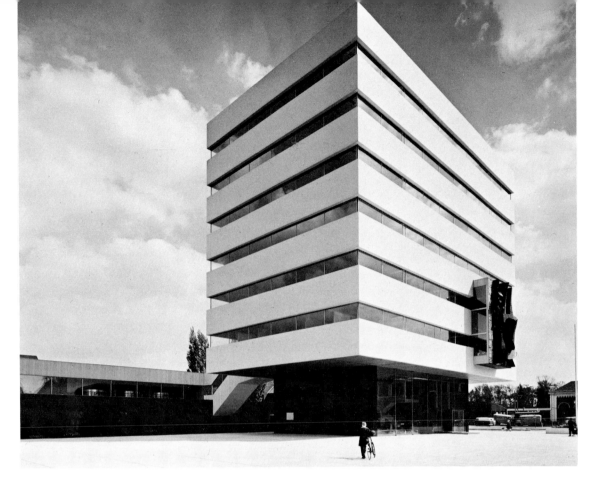

Above and Below left:
TOMADO OFFICE BUILDING, DORDRECHT, HOLLAND. *Architect*: Maaskant van Dommelen. *Artist*: Joop van den Broek, glass sculpture, 15' x 21'; 1962. *Photographer*: Foto Jan Versnel.

UNILEVER NV. BUILDING, ROTTERDAM, HOLLAND. *Architect*: A. J. B. van de Graaf. *Artist*: Wessel Couzijn, "Rhythm in Bronze," bronze sculpture; 1963. *Photographer*: Gerrit Burg.

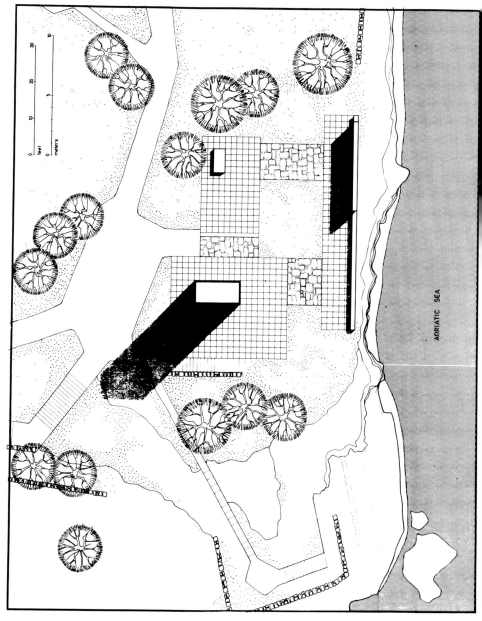

LIGHTHOUSE, SPLIT, YUGOSLAVIA. *Architect*: Ivan Caric. *Artist*: Andrija Krstulović, lighthouse, 120' high; rock, 48' high; sculpture, 23' x 9' x 16"; white limestone; 1958. *Photograph*: Courtesy of Ivan Caric.

The interest of this project, erected in memory of sailors, resides in the fact that this actual lighthouse, which indicates the entrance to the Port of Split, has become, because of its general concept and because of the integration of a sculpture, a monument.

The strong link between the function of the lighthouse and the sailor's everyday life is made evident by this work.

Ivan Caric

LIGHTHOUSE, SPLIT, YUGOSLAVIA. *Architect*: Ivan
Caric. *Artist*: Andrija Krstulović, lighthouse, 120' high;
rock, 48' high; sculpture, 23' x 9' x 16"; white limestone; 1958. *Photograph*: Courtesy of Ivan Caric.

COMMISSIONING THE ARTIST

Represented in this book are examples of collaboration between architects and artists, ranging from large Federal, state, and city projects to private homes. Although in some instances I have explained the procedures by which artists are commissioned, I thought it would be helpful to architects and artists to enumerate here in greater detail the necessary steps to be taken when the use of art is contemplated.

The most important thing is that there must be a mutual understanding between owner and architect of the necessity of incorporating art as part of the entire building concept and of budgeting an adequate amount of money for it.

There are several ways to secure the services of an artist. If the architect considers himself sufficiently knowledgeable in the art field, he may commission an artist who he feels could successfully handle the assignment. Presumably, this artist has performed well in the past and is dependable. Architect and artist should meet at the very inception of the project to discuss location, size, material, scale, and cost of the commission. It is necessary that the artist submit a scale model or drawing for approval by both the architect and the owner. At this point, the conflicts of art expression and concepts are apt to come to the fore. It is here that the architect should guide the owner in reaching an understanding and acceptance of the model. Should the preliminary model still be unacceptable, the artist may have to submit revised concepts until complete agreement is reached.

Another procedure of commissioning an artist is to have a limited competition by inviting three or four artists to submit their concepts in the form of models or sketches. In this instance, each artist is paid an agreed amount for his preliminary work. Often the understanding is that the successful competitor credits his preliminary remuneration to the total cost of the commission. Here again, the final choice is made by the architect and the owner.

Another method is to set up an art committee consisting of the architect, the owner or his representative, and several recognized art authorities, i.e., the director of a museum, the head of a university fine art department, the dean of an architectural school, or other persons in this field who are acceptable to the architect and the owner. The procedure thereafter is similar to that used in the aforementioned examples.

I suspect that one of the reasons why architects and owners shy away from considering art for their buildings is that they generally know only a few outstanding artists whose fees are higher than their budgets allow. The fact is, however, that there are many young and talented artists in every region who can be sought out to execute commissions. From my own experience I have found that these young artists, once given a chance, show competence and responsibility. In many cases, such a commission has been the first big step toward a successful art career. I am certain that this experience can be repeated in many parts of this country and elsewhere.

Another reason why architects are reluctant to consider work with artists is that a new responsibility is added to the many others they carry. With the many pressures of deadlines, budget limitations, etc., collaboration with an artist has to be a labor of love and a conviction that art is an essential part of the building concept. Some architects whose buildings suggest sculptural forms do not feel the necessity for adding or integrating other artwork. This may be well justified. It is also advisable to omit artwork where it only serves as a redeeming element in an otherwise poorly designed building.

Whether a new or an experienced artist is being engaged, there must always be a businesslike approach in reaching a working arrangement. The following items need to be considered:

1. Preparation of detailed specifications for the art work, similar to specifications for the building trades.

2. Guarantee by the artist of the permanency of materials used and of functional operation (as in case of fountains).

3. Definite arrangements for the installation of the art work on the premises.

4. Time limit for completion of the project.

5. Periodic visits by the architect to the artist's studio to check progress and to solve unforeseen problems.

Detailed specifications are a very important document for a clear understanding of the proper materials to be used, of the required finishes, and of all component parts, whether mechanical, electrical, or other. Good specifications make it possible to avoid misunderstanding and friction between the parties.

To protect the owner's interest, the artist should provide a written guarantee for a two-year period. The intent of this guarantee is to stimulate the artist to study the permanency of materials and, if necessary, to consult specialists in the field. This is especially important when art work is exposed to the weather regardless of climate. I know of one case in which the adhesive for a mosaic mural did not stand up in the cold of winter. A more thorough investigation of the properties of the adhesive as claimed by the manufacturer could have avoided this failure. A similar case of much greater proportions occurred in Mexico City. There thousands of square feet of mosaic tesserae had to be completely replaced because of faulty adhesive. The problem of permanency applies to many other materials, such as marble, welded steel, aluminum, paint finishes, and plastics.

As for the installation of the art work, the artist should be responsible for the delivery of his work in good condition on the premises but the installation itself should be handled by the general contractor's staff. Because the artist has limited contact with the various trades involved in the installation and because the general contractor has all the subtrades at his disposal, this procedure makes for a mutually satisfactory arrangement.

The time limit for completion of the art work is a very important factor. The completion of a building project is a big event in every owner's experience. The art work, which the owner has come to accept as a "luxury item" in his building costs, serves as an additional highlight in the opening festivities of the new building. It is obvious that lack of completion on time causes a big letdown for owner and architect alike.

It is important for the architect to keep in touch with the artist during the entire period, but especially in the beginning, when the general character of the composition begins to take shape. It happens frequently that the artist changes the concept quite radically on his own. Even though he should have freedom to develop the theme, the concept needs to be kept within the total architectural composition. The architect should visit the artist's studio periodically so that he can discuss the problems and, if required, assist the artist with his technical know-how.

I have tried in this book to emphasize only the major categories of art used in connection with buildings. There are other elements which should not be overlooked but which I have not stressed because of limitation of space. Such important elements are landscaping, paving patterns, lighting fixtures, fabrics, graphics, and sign work, all of which add to the integration and completeness of the overall concept of the building.

The reason this chapter deals in detail with the practical aspects of commissioning artists is that herein lies the basic element in achieving the aim of this book—the integration of art in architecture. A mutual understanding and an effective working relationship between architect and artist also serves as a bridge between the public and the artist.

This point is well illustrated with the commissioning of Pablo Picasso to create a sculpture for the Chicago Civic Center. After a period of many months of the architects' contacts with the artist to interest him in the project, a full accord was reached between them. The final result was summed up by the architects in a public statement: "It is remarkable that a city and an artist should have developed this astonishing affinity for one another; this mutual recognition of qualities for which they have both been extolled, derided, honored, criticized and enormously rewarded."[1]

In closing, I would like to say that the eternal quest of man for beauty will find its channels of expression in a multitude of art forms. It is a responsibility and a challenge to the architects and artists to heed this human need and do the utmost to create surroundings where art becomes an essential part of living.

[1] From a release by Public Buildings Commission of Chicago, Sept. 20, 1966.

INDEXES

INDEX OF ARCHITECTS

INDEX OF ARCHITECTS (Continued)

INDEX OF ARCHITECTS (Continued)

INDEX OF ARCHITECTS (Continued)

INDEX OF ARCHITECTS (Continued)

INDEX OF ARCHITECTS (Continued)

INDEX OF ARCHITECTS (Continued)

INDEX OF ARCHITECTS (Continued)

INDEX OF ARCHITECTS (Continued)

INDEX OF ARCHITECTS (Continued)

INDEX OF ARTISTS

INDEX OF ARTISTS (Continued)

INDEX OF PHOTOGRAPHERS

INDEX OF PHOTOGRAPHERS (Continued)

GENERAL INDEX

GENERAL INDEX (Continued)

GENERAL INDEX (Continued)

GENERAL INDEX (Continued)